Fire

a collection of stories, poems and visual images

Edited by Delys Bird

MARGARET RIVER
·PRESS·

ISBN: 978-0-9872180-7-0

First published in Australia
by Margaret River Press in 2013

P O Box 47
Witchcliffe
Western Australia 6286
www.margaretriverpress.com

Cataloguing-in-Publication data is available from
the National Library of Australia

ISBN:	978-0-9872180-7-0
Designer:	Tracey Gibbs
Editor:	Delys Bird
Printer:	Vanguard Press, Western Australia
Publisher:	Margaret River Press, Western Australia

Cover Photograph: Margaret River Fires
2011, Sean Blocksidge

Delys Bird is a Senior Honorary Research Fellow in the School of Humanities at The University of Western Australia. She is Chair of the Board of writingWA, and a long-time co-editor of *Westerly*. Currently one of the judges on the WA Premier's Book Awards, she has also been a judge of the TAG Hungerford Award for several years.

Acknowledgements

Margaret River Press thanks all those who submitted their work in response to our call for this anthology. Our heartfelt thanks to Delys Bird, who spent weeks selecting works and putting the whole publication together. It was a mammoth task. Thanks to the members of the Editorial Board of the Press for their assistance in the selection of a long list. Finally, we thank our wonderfully talented designer Tracey Gibbs.

Contents

introduction

The primal place that fire occupies in so many cultural contexts, histories and imaginaries is indicated by the response to the call for submissions to this anthology, making editing the volume both intensely interesting and challenging. Caroline Wood, publisher and director of Margaret River Press, and its editorial board read and considered over three hundred submissions before we made final decisions. We are also fortunate to have had access to the work of the 2013 exhibition on fire held at the Holmes à Court Gallery at Vasse Felix in Cowaramup near Margaret River. Sharon Tassicker, Curator at the Gallery, has written a brief Introduction, 'Fire: Some kind of energy' to that work for this volume. In it, she delineates the contradictory meanings of fire, writing: 'Fire is elemental and divine, useful and comforting, beautiful and terrible, destructive and transformative. It can result in trauma and loss ... [but also] reveal the strength and resilience ... of extraordinary people.' And we have been able to use extracts from oral histories recorded by the Margaret River and Districts Historical Society and the Margaret River Community Resource Centre with victims of the Margaret River fires of late 2011, among them statements from just such people.

A similar range of differing attitudes and responses to fire are contained in the poetry, fiction and visual material in this anthology. Some refer to contemporary events and are often realistic; others use legend, history and memory in their work. David Milroy's story, 'Walardu and Karla', was commissioned for the anthology. Set in the Kimberley, it draws on an Aboriginal legend of Karla, the fire that 'had burned for more than twenty years.' Karla is recognisable by the presence of Walardu, the eagle who is her partner. Written as a series of short tales, 'Walardu and Karla' evokes the bond between brothers Bailey and Alfred, the comfortable place they occupy in their landscape, and the way it speaks to them through signs like the appearance of Walardu and Karla, signifying both life and death. Legends and dreaming stories also provide material for depictions of aspects of fire in the paintings by the Aboriginal artists in the Holmes à Court exhibition, while others draw on direct, contemporary experience of bushfires as well as an ancient spiritual idea of fire.

Realistic, domestic reactions to the threat of fire are presented in two stories that follow. In 'Cool Change' Kate Rizzetti portrays a couple on the eve of their fiftieth wedding anniversary, after days of stifling heat and monitoring a fire that is coming closer to their home, disagreeing about what to do. Pat wants to go but Keith won't leave, and his stubbornness, even in the face of CFA directions to leave is very familiar to Pat. Françoise van der Plank's 'Getting on with Life' also explores the difficulty of making the decision to evacuate. Told in matter-of-fact prose that overlays the potential drama of the situation, Sara and Paul and their two young children prepare their house in the face of oncoming fire. They're uncertain and fearful; finally they go then return, to find their home intact, but surrounded by devastation.

Paul Hetherington's poem 'Bushfire' captures 'the aftermath of fire,' where 'nights [are] charred with recollection.' Although the 'local store piled its verandah/with new goods,' its generator leans 'where the fire had caught it,/ ... into black-toothed grimace.' Carmel Macdonald Grahame's 'Coming Down to Earth' is poised between the witty reconstruction of the experience of shopping for all the things our houses contain as a 'quest through unsettling displays/ of life's minutiae' and the serious, poignant purpose of this particular shopping, which is 'guided by necessity,' to replace the contents of a house that has 'subsid[ed] into an ash-bed.'

In 'Holyoake', Donna Mazza draws on the history of a fire in the district of Dwellingup in January 1961, reported in a 'Daily News account [as the] "worst night of terror in WA history as the inferno roared into the town."' 'Three concrete steps ... left on the side of a hill' are the only reminders of a family home and business. Mazza's character, Margaret, a small child at the time of the fire, tries to recreate her own history from these and other relics, and from her memory of escaping the fire. Heidi Trudinger's photographic record of objects found after the 2009 Black Saturday bushfires in Victoria, 'The Minutiae of Homes Lost', takes up the idea of the significance of such found objects. They become 'fragments of stories and memories'; reminders too of the potential of fire to remake, as myth and legend, history and memory do.

Using a mixture of historical research and creative re-imagining, Cassandra Atherton's 'Raining Blood and Money: Remembering the Triangle Shirtwaist Fire' is a response to a tragic fire in a clothing factory in Milwaukie in 1911 in the US, in which 146 people died in eighteen minutes. That fire and its death toll were the result of gross negligence and of practices that meant workers were 'entombed in the building.' Another historical event, the legendary stand of the Kelly gang against the forces of the law, is the background to Dorothy Simmons' 'No Surrender'. Her poetic retelling of a familiar tale adopts Kelly's mother's perspective. As an old woman in Australia, Ellen Kelly remembers telling her grown children a story her Da told her as a child in Ireland, of the Protestant people of Derry who held out in the famous seventeenth-century siege of their town. Their slogan 'no surrender' is one she has made her sons swear to.

Both Judy Johnson's 'At Glendalough Monastery' and Michelle Leber's 'The Great Kiln' recall events of the past. In Johnson's poem, the burnt-out monastery is a reminder of ancient burnings that have left their mark, yet 'Glendalough makes no distinction/between the ash of now/and the sixth century.' Leber adopts a persona, in 'the voice of The Yellow Emperor – 17th Century BCE, China,' who watches 'moths fly out of my whiskers/to settle on the hearth,' leading him to a symbolic understanding, perhaps, that moving 'toward the fire' involves necessary renunciation. While Miranda Aitken's concrete poem 'Isaac's Land Is Burning' seems to recall ancient myth in its title, it also refers to Isaac's Ridge, the name of a place in Margaret River. The urgency conveyed by the poem's single- or double-word lines matches its topic, fleeing the danger of fire.

The history of the Second World War is central to Jo

Gardiner's 'Firestorm'. Nineteen-year-old Hana's experience of the murderous firestorm created by American bombers over Tokyo in March 1945, is contrasted with the beauty of the 'garden cultivated by neglect' where Hana waits, 'beneath skeins of wild geese calling ... in a pond of darkness.' Later, living in Australia as a war bride, Hana has a Japanese garden, against which the Australian bush presses, until a bushfire destroys everything but that garden. In 'Lamprey' Aksel Dadswell presents a futuristic landscape as apocalyptic as that of war-ravaged Tokyo. Dadswell's story opens with a sex, drugs and alcohol-fuelled beach party. The 'arson-based shenanigans' of the narrator's friends appear to be a response to what remains an unexplained disaster, but the moral emptiness of this reaction leads him to compare the revelers to the parasitic lamprey, that attach themselves to a host fish and feed off its living tissues.

The awful capacity of fire to ravage is also the topic of Peter Hill's photographic essay, 'Why Would you Want to Walk in Such Devastation?'. This question directs his walk through a fire-damaged landscape three months after the Babbington fire near Northcliffe. His answer lies in his 'awe and wonder' at the ways the bush responds to fire. Janet Jackson, too, celebrates the endurance of the natural world in her poem, 'The alkali cleansing'. The 'charcoal and ash' left by fire has that cleansing effect, leading to rebirth. Karen Throssell uses extracts from public fire warnings and CFA checklists among her poetic fragments in 'Alert Message (North Warrandyte Feb. 7th 2009)', presenting an idea of the chaos experienced by those in a fire-threatened area, as they must 'Learn[ing] a new language': "Ember attacks" "Alert messages".'

Two stories about young people are very different in subject matter and style. In 'The Pressure Suit', Brooke Dunnell deals with a young boy injured in a domestic fire in which his mother and baby brother perish while he watches helplessly. Returning to school after months of skin grafts and outer healing, he wears a pressure suit on his injured arm, a reminder of his terrible loss. Claire Dunn's 'Quest for Fire' has a very morally sound first-person narrator, a young woman who is on a year-long retreat in the wilderness as a member of an 'Independent Wilderness Study Programme.' The pretension of the idea of living a 'solo wilderness reverie' is brought out by the narrative irony as she struggles to make a fire without matches.

Moya Pacey invokes a domestic memory of 'Building Fire', as a mother demonstrates how to make a fire, recalling the mother's past resourcefulness: 'If there's no wood, she'll burn/old shoes – one winter she chopped the upright piano/...

piece/by shiny wooden piece-.' Rachel Mead's 'The Water Tanks' relates how a farmer's care of his water tanks is repaid when his 'wife and kids with no time/for the road or the sprinklers' find shelter from a bushfire 'in the tiny cross between the tanks.'

Interviews from the report into the 2011 Margaret River fires include reminders of the arbitrary nature of fire, an example of which was the loss of the privately owned historic home Wallcliffe House, while another regional landmark, the tiny white Greek Chapel of St John at Prevelly, remained unscathed in a burnt-out landscape. Unexpected and shocking, the fires resulted in chaotic responses and the effects of this experience is palpable in the way people have described it. On the other hand, the possibility of regeneration is the preoccupation of 'Black & White and Colour', Mike Rumble's photographic essay. His photos of this process, taken after the Margaret River fires, recall both 'the natural beauty and power of the fire' and the recovery of the bush after fire.

Memories of fire and storm inform a visit to 'South West Cape, the endpoint of a continent' in Beverley Lello's poem 'The Return'. There, the landscape carries the imprint of those natural elements, yet it is those who visit that invest ‘this place’ with ‘our tales.’ And in ‘Playing with Fire’ (also commissioned for this volume), Miriam Wei Wei Lo explores several ways in which fire informs people’s lives, both literally and symbolically, across different cultural contexts and times. Among them are a family’s funeral rites, where ‘they burn paper houses for the next life -’; the aftermath ‘of the small Gracetown fire’; and the conflicted nature of love, wordless ‘after consummation’ when ‘Love and Anger [are] lying so close/together on the bed.’

Finally, Maurie Roche brings together his past and present experiences of fire, recalling in ‘Untitled’ the first time he witnessed bushfire - in 1968 at Manly in Sydney as a newly arrived migrant from Ireland. Now living in Margaret River, his photographs of that fire in 2011 are his attempt, he writes, to ‘show ... awe and respect for nature’s fire.’

walardu and karla

David Milroy

Murandoo

A Murandoo bathed in the final embers of the day, unaware that its blood-red anthill platform had unmasked its speckled camouflage. Bailey slammed on the brakes and leapt from his Toyota, chasing the lizard across the dry riverbed and up onto the bank. Before it could scurry into a hole he grabbed its tail and whacked it against a snappy gum.

On the ride home he celebrated his kill with a Slim Dusty cassette while on the backseat the Murandoo's cold-blooded heart was being kick started by the vibrations of the corrugated road. With a spark in its tiger-eye it leapt into the front seat and flung itself at the windscreen. With lightning

reflexes Bailey gripped it to his chest, unwilling to let his dinner escape through the passenger-side window.
He flew into his brother's camp emerging from a cloud of red dust desperately trying to wrench the Murandoo's claws from his faded Dockers jumper. With flaying arms he ripped it free and threw it to the ground. Alfred pulled himself out from under the bull buggy and caught the last rock-thumping hit to the Murandoo's head.

He don't wanna die!

With the last twitch of its tail the life drained from their dinner.

Under the hat

That night Bailey took his time preparing it for the coals. Alfred sat by the fire with his hat pulled low over his brow, lost in thought. He was worrying for his wife Marjorie. She'd been flown to Perth for medical tests. With every sip of his tea, he was counting the days till she returned. His mood was momentarily broken when Bailey snapped a twig into a harpoon and with deadly precision stuck it up the Murandoo's arse. With a couple of twists he pulled out the guts and flicked them to the dogs. One by one he twisted the

Murandoo's legs until...
Snap!
There's nothing worse than a Murandoo standing up in the fire!
Snap!
She's a good woman, Marjorie.
Snap!
I've never been lucky in love like you Alfred.
Snap!
You found the right one, first time!

Alfred stroked his beard and retreated further under his hat. This was not the brother that Bailey knew. Normally he couldn't compete with Alfred's ability to spin a good yarn, and if he did he could always go one better. Bailey had one ace left up his sleeve so he scraped open the fire, raked the coals over the Murandoo and played his hand.

I seen old Karla today.

Alfred raised the brim of his hat.

How do you know it was her?

One fire, one eagle and they was heading this way!

Alfred removed his hat.

Maybe she wanna tell us something.

Hmmm!

Bailey, looking forward to spending a night eating and yarning with his brother, hurriedly pulled their dinner from the coals and placed it on a table of leaves. Unfortunately Alfred had lost his appetite for Murandoo and conversation. With a flick of his wrist he threw the last dregs of tea from his panikin and headed for his swag.

Muddy Water

Earlier that week Alfred and Bailey had dug a new soak. They let it fill up overnight and rose early the next day to fill the tank. Alfred worked the generator while Marjorie stood high on the platform balancing the irrigation pipe on her shoulder. Bailey stood below taking the full weight of the pipe so she could wrestle it into position. She aimed the pipe and with a wave of her hand signaled for Alfred to start the pump. With a puff of black smoke it rattled into life filling the old tank with muddy water. Once the water was flowing Marjorie reached to tie the pipe to the ladder but slipped and dropped the wire. She was unsteady on her feet. The ladder swayed as her foot slid from the rung.

I'm...I'm...

Her voice could hardly be heard over the rattle of the pump. With a last desperate grab at the ladder she hit the side of the tank and fell like a ragdoll to the ground. For a moment she sat up then collapsed back into the mud of the overflow. Alfred cut the pump and within minutes they were driving flat out along the dusty track into town. At the nursing post they sat anxiously watching the clock tick by as the nurse examined Marjorie. Her diagnosis was swift.

I think it's your kidneys but you'll need more tests in Perth to make sure.

The nurse filled in the forms and worked the phones.

The Flying Doctor's on its way!

Alfred held Marjorie's hand and struggled to give her a reassuring smile knowing she'd never been to Perth or flown in a plane before. At the airstrip, the nurse loaded her onboard, carefully handing the drip to the Flying Doctor nurse. The shadow of the plane cut through Alfred as it left the runway. In an instance the Flying Doctor had separated the inseparable, and stolen his first and only love from his side. On the solemn trip back to camp Bailey's dusty cassettes lay scattered on the floor and no song of Slim's was going to bring comfort to Alfred.

Walardu and Karla

Bailey had decided to stay with his brother until Marjorie returned. He knew she liked bush tucker so every day he rose with the shadows, loaded the Jillyman and headed bush. After doing the full length of Quartz road without an animal in sight he headed for Bullocky Spring. Ten miles out he spotted Karla cutting through the spinifex. He'd never seen Karla before but knew all the legends surrounding her. Karla was the fire that had burned for more than twenty years, sometimes disappearing for months then rising out of nowhere. Karla could travel underground and was more lightning than fire, but what set Karla apart from other fires was her partner.

Spook was the local expert on the Karla legend and also the local barfly. He had, like many old leathery drifters, settled in the most isolated town in the Norwest, happy to live the rest of his life in beer, in cigarettes and in-cognito. Spook had the ability to combine legends with theories and it was this ability that had got him into trouble with the Queensland police, something to do with peppering an old mine with a shotgun blast of gold. Spook would always start with a crocodile yarn to attract the unsuspecting tourist. Then he'd order a pint, re-adjust his barstool and launch into his legendary Karla Lege-theory.

When they stopped culling crocs in the Kimberley, the bulls headed south in search of new nesting grounds. One morning Walardu the eagle sat by the river tearing through the fur of a quoll with its razor beak. She threw back her head and swallowed the flesh, unconcerned about the still waters of the De Grey.

Snap! A croc flung from the water!

Spook liked that part of the legend because he could usually get the tourists to jump by clapping his hands together then he'd con them into shouting him another beer for his parched throat so he could finish the yarn. After sculling his pint he'd abandon the barstool and play out the story for what it was worth.

The croc was over ten metres long and luckily for Walardu took more feathers than bone. The wounded Walardu flew high into the sky but the adrenalin faded and she slowly spiraled to the ground below. Suddenly she felt a warm updraft lifting her body. Beneath her Karla the spinifex fire burned and the one winged Walardu could fly again.

Walardu and Karla!

The eagle the fire!
Then with a tear in Spook's bloodshot eye he'd head for the barstool and call out.

One more pint for the storyteller!

The Moth

From his swag Alfred watched the stars dance with the satellites, searching for enough comfort to fall asleep. He reached across to where Marjorie usually lay and touched the air, imagining the softness of her skin and the shadow of her back. He pulled her pillow close to his body and dreamt of better times.

The first time they met was under a night sky. There was a party in town travelling on the wind. The music was fading in and out, just enough to attract a young moth like Alfred. With a swig of his king brown beer he followed the music to One-Mile camp, only to be told the party had moved on. He put his ear to the night sky and headed to Five Mile, again missing them by minutes. Reluctantly, with an empty tank and a bladder full of beer he headed back to town. On the way home he pulled over for a piss, as the mist rose from the ground he caught the faint music of the boom box falling from the heavens and calling him to Blackhorse Pool.

His Holden squeaked along the river track in search of the party. Alfred scanned the banks for signs of life and was about to call it a night when in the distance he spotted the light of a solitary cigarette. He casually dismounted his HQ Holden wagon and with thumbs tucked into his buckle approached the girls with a gunslinger swagger.

What you mob up to?

Fuck off!

Before he had time to draw his breath they'd shot him out of his cowboy boots and snapped his buckle clean off.

Under the volley of abuse he retreated to his HQ wagon, happy to give up on his moth-driven quest for loving. He sat in his car sipping the last of his beer and planning his face-saving burnout. Then from out of the darkness there came the voice of a goddess.

Ya got any cigarettes?

He turned slowly to face his destiny.

Nup! Don't smoke.

Her eyes sparkled like amethyst on the darkest sea.

Me neither.

Her words shot like shooting stars into his ears.

Ya wanna go for a cruise?

His heart pounded like the waves of a winter storm.

Yer, why not!

Alfred and Marjorie rode off into the sunrise with their desires overflowing like stuffing from the crack in his backseat.

Snowflake

Alfred settled into courting Marjorie in true Jackaroo style determined to impress her with his prowess as a broncobuster. The rodeo had hit town and the ten thousand-dollar prize money would get him a deposit on the block he'd been eyeing off with the same twinkle he had for Marjorie. His dream was to set up his own mustering business using bull buggies instead of horses, which were rapidly becoming obsolete as the stations became more mechanized. Riding on his prowess as a broncobuster was not only the prize money, but also the quest for Marjorie's heart.

All eyes were on the swing gate, where on the other side of the fence, Alfred sat squeezing the bronco between his legs and gripping the rigging with his leather glove. His allocated bronco had recently received legendary status by throwing Knuckles Dan, one of the most prominent outback riders on the rodeo circuit, in three seconds. The horse was called Snowflake because of its white hide, but after what it had done to Knuckles it was renamed Ball Buster.

The announcements echoed across the crowd, re-living the highlights of Snowflake's new-found fame and taunting the young buck Alfred who was supposedly going to melt the ball-busting Snowflake into the dust of the rodeo ground. The swing gate opened and Snowflake leapt sideways from the chute causing Marjorie's heart to pump faster than a windmill in a cyclone. Alfred had to stay on for eight seconds to win the money. The eight seconds seemed like minutes as Snowflake flung forward then backwards trying to throw Alfred over her snowy mane. He held on tight throwing his arm high in the air to counter balance the heaving mass of horseflesh beneath him. Snowflake kicked back and shook from side to side trying to throw him but the determined Alfred gripped tight to the rigging with his sweaty glove, unwilling to be another notch on Snowflake's saddle. In one last desperate attempt to dislodge Alfred, Snowflake bolted to the perimeter of the rodeo ground and slammed against the railing. The crowd gasped then wondered if the crack they'd heard was Snowflake's ribs, Alfred's leg or the railing. The eight-second siren had long gone and Alfred, unaware that he'd won the money, was prised from the busted bronco. Lying on a stretcher beneath his hat, Alfred was comforted by the thought that a broken leg was much less painful than a broken heart.

The Whirlpool of Darkness

Bailey was scared of snakes so every night he raked the ground before he went to sleep. In the morning he'd check to see what had crawled through the camp. He raked together a small pile of stones and looked towards his brother's swag. He felt helpless knowing his brother was cut deep and the only cure would be the return of Marjorie.

The night drifted into an indigo darkness that stole Alfred's thoughts and wrought them into a whirlpool of dreams. His dreams travelled far, visiting old friends he'd never met before and strangers who spoke warmly of Alfred's love for Marjorie. His stomach rippled as their words filled him with hope. Soon his dream grew weary and their words faded into the sound of a crackling fire. He looked to a shadow that flickered in the firelight at his feet, he lifted his head and there standing before him was Marjorie. She was younger and smiling as she showed him her sickness had gone. As a shy wind blew across the camp Marjorie faded into the night and the whirlpool of dreams took Alfred back into his sleep beneath the satellite sky.

Mobile Morning

Bailey poured fuel down the drop toilet. He knew if they left the burn-off too late the wind would pick up and they'd be stalked all day by the smell of shit and petrol fumes. Unfortunately he'd used a little too much fuel and the blast blew the seat of the toilet high into the sky. Alfred shot out of his swag, taking a moment to register where the explosion had come from.

It's okay! I'll find ya another seat!

Alfred rubbed the sleep from his eyes then searched for Marjorie's footprints in the raked over ground. There were no signs of a visit. He sat solemn by the morning fire searching for the courage to tell his brother of his night travels. Bailey broke the silence.

I smelt smoke last night but there was no fire.

Alfred adjusted the brim of his hat then, with head down, told Bailey of being visited by the young healthy Marjorie. He then retreated under his hat trying to hide the tears that fell onto the dusty red dirt. Bailey searched his jacket for his car keys.

Let's drive up to Razor Ridge and see if we can get some reception.

Bailey waited at the foot of the rise as Alfred climbed his way up on to the ridge. At the top he held his arm out moving the phone from side to side trying to pick up a signal. At first there was only one bar, then two, and then the beep of a message. Alfred took a deep breath and pressed the callback.

Yes, yes it's me Alfred, Marjorie's husband.

Alfred paced the ridge with the phone glued to his ear. He slowly dropped the phone and drifted to the ground, wounded by the call.

The land was warming to the morning sun and a light breeze gathered over the ridge. To the east, Alfred could see his corrugated tin camp shining like a speck of gold in the vast red landscape. He looked to the distant horizon where a spinifex fire burned and gently raised his hand to wave goodbye to his love.

fire: some kind of energy

Sharon Tassicker

It was a coincidence that we were planning an exhibition about fire when Margaret River Press approached us early in 2012 about contributing to this volume. When we purchased Joseph Tjangala Zimran's painting, *Fire Dreaming* in August 2011, I commented that we had enough works in the collection with fire as their subject to make a quite spectacular exhibition. Some months later the Margaret River fires raged out of control, Janet's front door caught alight, homes and property were destroyed, the community was devastated and suddenly everything became much more serious. We took sober and sympathetic note of the community response, including that of artists, added some pertinent pieces to the art collection and reached out in order to incorporate some of the community experience into the exhibition plan. We didn't pull back from making the exhibition, believing that an exhibition space can provide the time and place for quiet consideration, reflection and healing.

Fire is problematic. It has been with us for 470 million years. Wildfires were first recorded in the fossil record 420 million years ago and became more prevalent 6-7 million years ago when grasses became dominant components of many ecosystems. Fire is elemental and divine, useful and comforting, beautiful and terrible, destructive and transformative. It can result in trauma and loss, generating anger, sadness, bitterness and resignation. Fire can also reveal the strength and resilience, the heroic and hopeful nature of extraordinary people.

Images of fire will usually depict some kind of energy – positive, negative or neutral. Some common symbolic fire associations are passion, extreme emotions, fever, destructive attitudes, greed, hate and anger. On the more positive side, fire can symbolise transformation, also prayer, meditation and contemplation. Images of flames can be about love, truth to self, spirituality, search for self and self- knowledge.

The following images and the stories attached to them were included in the exhibition. They help illustrate some of the myriad qualities, associations, symbols and emotions that fire generates.

Creation and the Divine

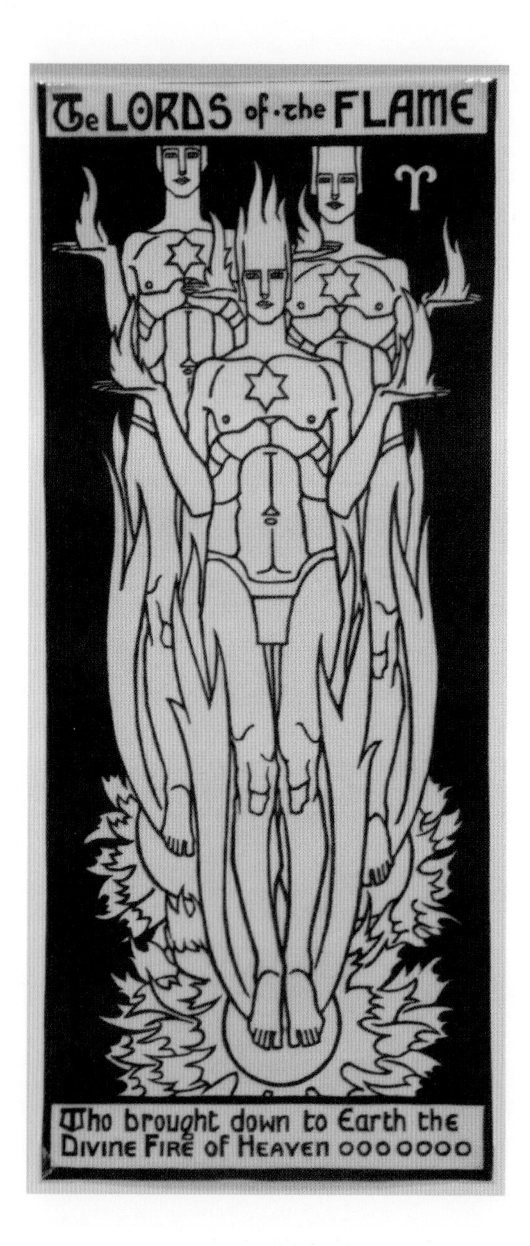

Christian Waller

The Lords of the Flame 1932

Linocut

31.4 x 13.5 cm

Janet Holmes à Court

Collection

Copyright and courtesy

Napier Waller House

Committe of Management

Christian Waller
The Lords of the Flame 1932

Theosophists, of whom Christian Waller was one, believed that Sanat Kumara, the great guru and saviour of earth, came from the planet Venus with the Lords of the Flame, who included Christ and the Buddha, to set up his colony. They brought with them an indeterminate number of souls. It is maintained in most versions of Theosophy that Venus is the most spiritually advanced planet of our solar system. Its beings are said to be hundreds or millions of years ahead of us in their spiritual evolution. The Lords of the Flame brought Love to earth and other precious gifts. The flames in this image denote that love Divine. [1]

(1) http://en.wikipedia.org/w/index.php?title=Sanat_Kumara&oldid=509275768

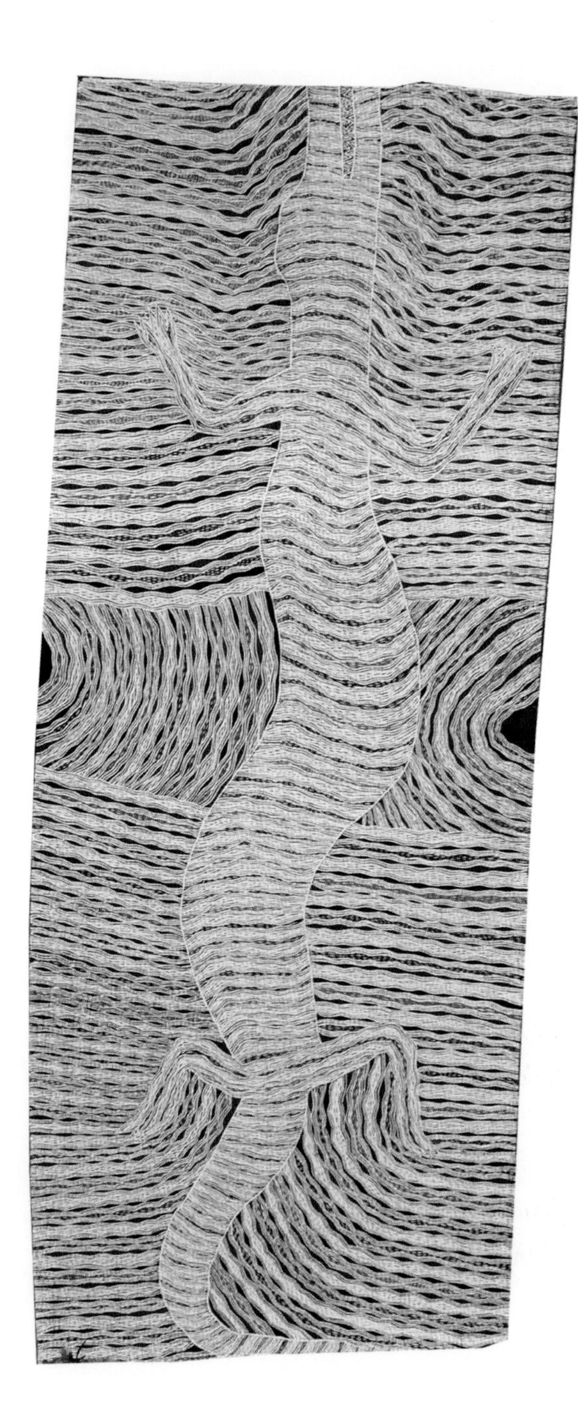

Djambawa Marawili
Garrangali 2005
Earth pigments on bark
207 x 79 cm
Janet Holmes à Court Collection

Djambawa Marawili

Garrangali

Djambawa explains the elements of his painting as themes of fire and water and describes the ancestral events in which Baru, the crocodile, plays a central role. The open ended strings of diamonds marks the classic miny'tji of the saltwater estate of Yathikpa. Here Baru the ancestral crocodile, carrying and being burnt by the Ancestral Fire crossed the beach from Garrangali and entered the saltwater. Baru decided after being soothed of his burns that he would stay in these waters. His sacred powers in line with that of the fire imbues the water there today. Crocodiles generally remain in the water and stay away from fire even today. The scarring on their bodies recalling those earlier burns. This painting relates to landforms in Madarrpa country and to ancestral events tied in with this land belonging to Madarrpa people. The miny'tji or sacred clan design on this work depicts the Fire and the sacred waters of Garrangali. The waters are sacred because, as the Madarrpa will tell you, they are from this water and upon death and through appropriate ritual they will return to this font of Madarrpa ancestral souls.

Garrangali is protected, as a special place of significance, for the Madarrpa by the intense heat of the lingering Ancestral Fire, and the real presence of Baru protecting its nests. This black soil is too hot to walk on in the breeding season of Baru even for the toughest Yolngu feet, further proof of the fire within the land.

Story courtesy the artist,
Madarrpa clan and
Buku-Larrnggay Mulka Art Centre

Control, warmth, comfort and protection

Jimmy Pike
Two men sleeping by two fires 1985
Black on white screen print
31.5 x 37.6 cm
Janet Holmes à Court Collection

Jimmy Pike
Two men sleeping by two fires 1985

These two old men are sleeping by two fires. They have made a windbreak all around and are curled up. They are cousin-brothers, Parnaparnti and Kurntumaru. Kurntumaru is the black goanna that hides in trees. Parnaparnti is the yellow sand goanna.

Beauty, terror and the colour of heat

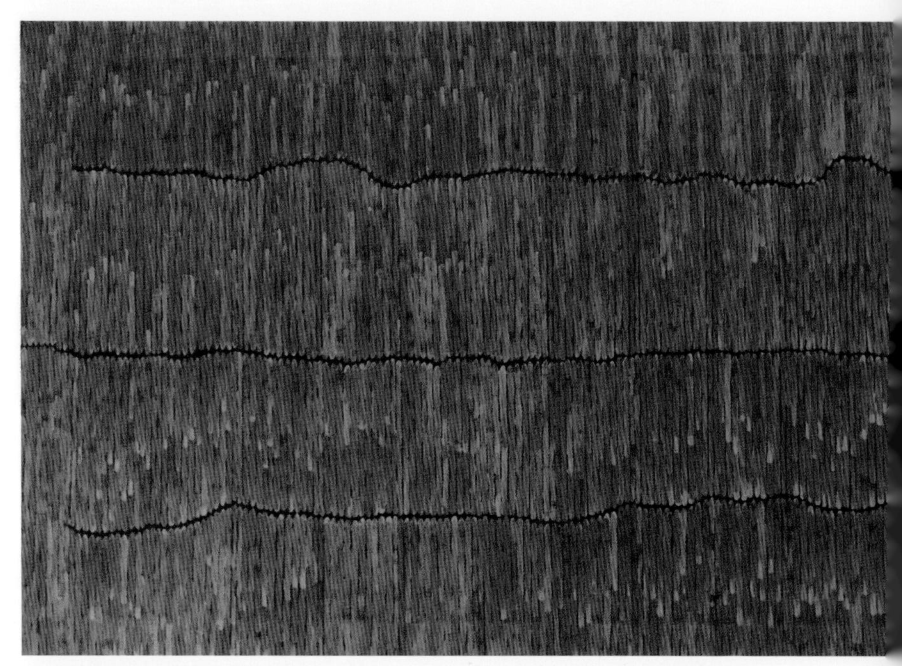

Joseph Tjangala Zimran
Waru Tjukurrpa (Fire Dreaming) 2011
Acrylic on Belgian linen
100 x 180 cm
Janet Holmes à Court Collection
Copyright and courtesy the artist

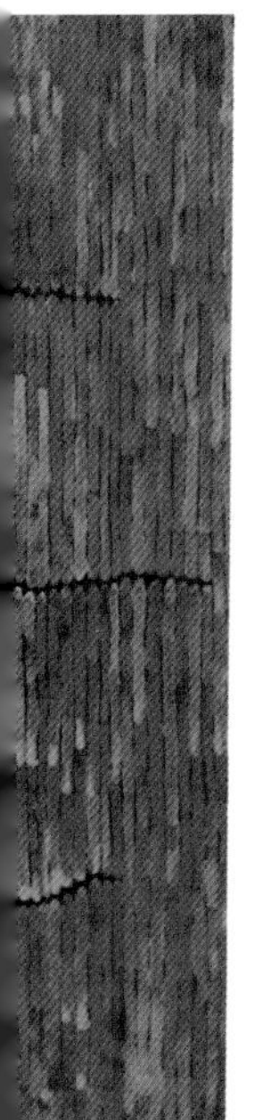

Joseph Tjangala Zimran

Waru Tjukurrpa (Fire Dreaming) 2011

Bush fire dreaming. This dreaming was passed down to me from my father. It is about when three big bushfires travelled across the land.They left big scars as they burnt the dry scrub that was spread across the sand dunes. In this painting it shows the burning fires.

Note: The dominant colour in a flame changes with temperature. Near the ground, where most burning is occurring, the fire is white, the hottest colour possible for organic material in general, or yellow. Above the yellow region, the colour changes to orange, which is cooler, then red, which is cooler still. Above the red region combustion no longer occurs, and the un-combusted carbon particles are visible as black smoke.[2]

(2) p.3 http://en.wikepedia.org/w/index.php?title=Fire&oldid=502863072

John Gollings

Aerial King Lake – Black Saturday 2009

Colour print on photo rag paper

95 x 142 cm

Janet Holmes à Court Collection

Copyright and courtesy the artist

John Gollings

Aerial King Lake – Black Saturday 2009

The red strokes in this bushfire image are the residual ash from burnt out and fallen limbs and trunks of a particular genus of pine tree whose ash is red/orange. Pine is less dense than other timbers, burns hotter but for a shorter time with many volatile components, which accounts for the particular colour. I was alerted to this information by the helicopter pilot who had been involved in the water bombing of the Victorian bushfires. In two hours of flying over all the burnt forests from that particular event this small stand of trees was unique. I have not found any other mention of this phenomenon in the published literature on bushfires and would of course be happy to be corrected! The image is an un-manipulated camera original except for a small increase in contrast and red saturation.

Power, vengeance and destruction

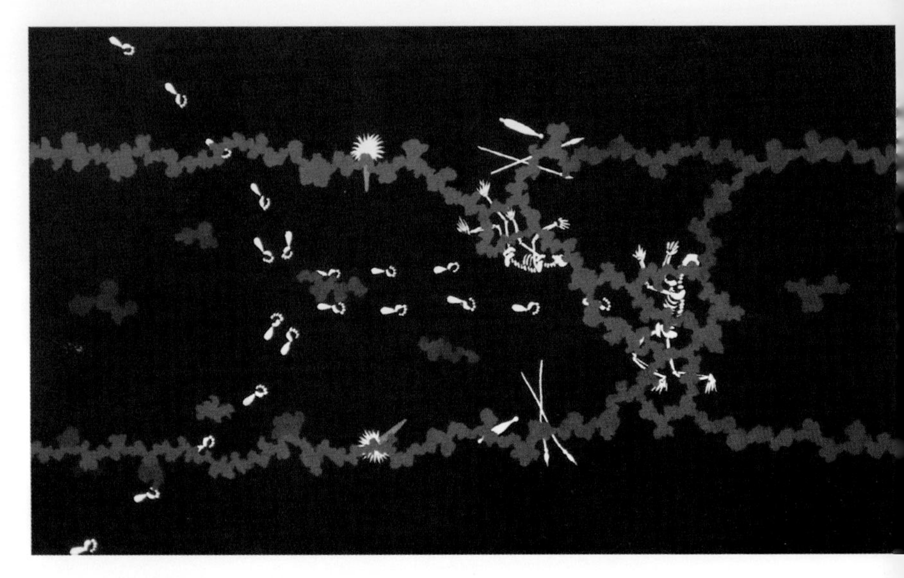

Clifford Possum Tjapaltjarri

Bush fire Dreaming 1988

Synthetic polymer paint on linen

170 x 287 cm

Janet Holmes à Court Collection

Clifford Possum Tjapaltjarri

Bush fire Dreaming 1988

The painting shows the skeletons of the two Tjampitjinpa brothers who perished at the site of Ramarakujunu ('red bones') in the great bushfire lit by Lungkata, the Blue Tongue Lizard Man, at Warlugulong. Lungkata, the Blue Tongue Lizard Man rested at the site of Warlugulong (approximately 300 kms north-west of Alice Springs), the site where the great fire began. His two sons, following behind, speared a kangaroo, cooked it, and then greedily ate it all. The father, wondering why his sons were so long, suddenly sensed what had happened. Determined to punish them, he blew on a firestick until it glowed, then touched it to a bush. The bush exploded into flame, then burnt everything in its path. Even though they were fighting the flames, the brother's perished far to the south.

The brothers fleeing footprints are shown heading back from the south as the fire comes around behind them. Their spears, spear throwers and bunches of sticks they used to try and beat out the fire are also shown, enveloped in a pall of grey smoke. The painting remains 'unfinished' as the artist did not apply the 'dotting' overlay that commonly conceals the narrative or story.

Human impact, anger, sadness, loss

Christine Gregory
Lost 2011-2012
Digital print, dyed and stitched fabric
32.5 x 150 cm
Janet Holmes à Court Collection
Copyright and courtesy the artist.

Christine Gregory

Lost 2011-2012

'Lost' reflects the environment immediately after the fire.
Everything was a shade of black, white or grey.
Sharp pointy sticks stuck out of the ash, like exclamation points on the shock and heartbreak felt by all when it was safe for locals to drive back into Prevelly.
Gone was the beautiful sheoak tree archway on my favourite track to the beach, gone was the pretty bush landscape alongside the cycle ways, gone was the environment for all the animals usually inhabiting the area, gone was the entire bush on the coastal dunes, for miles.
On certain days to follow, even the ocean would be full of ash, blown in off the dunes, and destroying the one thing that brought me happiness in otherwise charred surroundings.

Lost were my neighbours' homes and all their possessions.
Directly across the road, four houses in complete devastation.
Fences burnt and guttering flame stained, the house I rented had very nearly joined them.
I thanked my angels for watching over me, I thanked anyone who had helped, but mainly I gave thanks for the local fire brigades, who were so very brave.

I cried tears of relief to discover everything I owned still untouched inside. I had been at work at the time of the fire, and all I had was my handbag and the dress I had worn that day. I had been lucky to have a local resident (to whom I will be eternally grateful) rescue my beloved thirteen-year-old golden retriever as police refused to let me or anyone in that Wednesday afternoon. One of my neighbours had not even been allowed in to get his daughter who was home alone. I cannot fathom how horrendous that must have been. Thankfully, she was able to retreat to a friend of the family's house and in the end, was safe.

I cried tears of guilt, shame and sadness for those who had not been so lucky. I drove around for months after, with all my most important possessions in the car. Even today, at the slightest chance of a lightning storm, or witnessing a drift of smoke from any burning off, I still find myself quietly terrified, and back in the car go my things, along with my dog.

Lost is my sense of safety, and trust in DEC's ability to do their job competently. Waves of anger crept over me in the weeks to come after the fire, a so-called 'controlled burn' on one of the windiest, hottest weeks of the year. I was dumbfounded to learn from a friend in the SES, who had been helping fill water bomber planes during the fire, that one of the pilots had told her they were turned away by DEC from the initial fire scene at

Ellenbrook, saying it was 'under control'. Local brigades had also been turned away on several locations.
It all could have been prevented.

I wrote a petition requesting DEC's burning procedures must be revised, signed by hundreds of people.
I received polite letters in return from various departments and officials, promising of course, nothing.
I was dismayed to observe the Keelty enquiry was 'focused down', and deeply offended for the people who had been severely affected, when they were only offered a pathetic amount of compensation.

Ventilation, healing, transformation, hope

Community art exhibition at Rifle Butts Reserve, Prevelly, 2011 - 2012 (detail).
Curator Mark Heussenstamm.
Photo: Sue-Lyn Aldrian-Moyle

Community art exhibition at
Rifle Butt Reserve, Margaret River. 2011
Curator Mark Heussenstamm.

This exhibition is part of a process. We all need it to move on.
Mark Heussenstamm.

Note: Mark lost his studio, the art therein and his family home of thirty years in the Margaret River fire on Thursday 24 November 2011.

My thanks to the artists who have shared their stories, both personal and cultural. They illuminate understanding of aspects of fire, its energies and its continuing impact.

cool change

Kate Rizzetti

Heat prickled against Pat's skin like Keith's unshaven kiss. She stood on the crisping grass of her front yard watching butterflies of ash land in the palm of her hand. The air wrapped around her tight, like a blanket, stifling breath. The swollen flesh of her feet oozed out between the straps of her white vinyl sandals. She knew she should be wearing boots, Keith had told her more than once, but it was just too darned hot. Besides, if they had to leave she didn't want to spend the night and next day in cumbersome boots.

Pat glanced at the old Volvo sitting inert and useless in the driveway. For the third time in her sixty-nine years she wished she'd learned to drive. The first time was when Sally tore a gash across her thigh while playing on some old corrugated iron. The second was when her father was taken by a heart attack and Keith was away cutting timber. The third was now.

Above, tarnished sunlight filtered through a veil of smoky cloud. Pat fanned herself weakly, her hand barely making a breeze. She looked up through the strange air toward the mountain that loomed dark behind the house. It seemed small under the kingdom of blue-grey clouds towering above it. Smoke. Lumpy chunks of it climbing one on top of the other.

Keith appeared on the veranda, carrying a bucket in each hand. Water sloshed over the sides, making wet splodges in the dust. If she wasn't so grouchy she'd laugh. He was lanky under his long sleeved shirt, the two plastic buckets dangling like useless weapons. She looked at the bruised smoke-clouds, then back at Keith's buckets. Pat knew better than to take Keith head on. It was better to wear him down with nagging. Trouble is there's no time for that nonsense right now.

Keith put the buckets at either end of the veranda and came to stand at the top of the steps.

'What're you doing, love? I thought I told you to get the hose.'

Pat studied her husband. Other people saw him as a stubborn and difficult man, but she knew it was pride that made him the way he was. It had always been easier to give in to him, because he always thought he was right. From the moment they were engaged she had resigned herself to his 'better' judgement. She'd let him make all the big decisions – where they lived, whether she worked, how many kids. Whether to stay or leave.

Keith was staring at her, getting impatient. Pat turned toward the hose coiled near the front fence. The dry grass turned to dust as she walked. The hose was limp with heat when she picked it up, hanging in her hand like a dead thing. She looked into the sky to the hot ball-bearing of sun burning behind the streaky layers of cloud and smoke.

Forty years in the bush and she still wasn't used to it. The coarse and dusty smell of drying eucalyptus on these hot days, the slow pace of the world as it warmed up, the monotony of the people around her. She'd never stopped missing the city, the constant change, the distant rush of traffic, the click of heels on a footpath and those cool southerly changes rushing in across Port Phillip Bay. Civilisation had never been far away from the protection of the flyscreens in her bayside suburban home where she'd grown up. She'd traded all that security, all that sureness, for this vast, frightening landscape that filled her windows and this man of the mountain, as strong and unyielding as the gums he felled for a living.

Keith had taken the hose from her and turned it on. He directed a limp stream of water at the walls of the house. The drops dried in minutes, the hungry air sucking away the moisture.

'Darl, I think we should leave.'

Keith turned off the tap and returned to the veranda. The old wicker chair complained as he sat down and struggled with the laces on his heavy work boots.

'We've already been through this, love.' His was voice impatient. 'We can't leave. We've got to be ready for tomorrow.'

Pat fidgeted with her wedding ring. Yes, of course Keith would be concerned about tomorrow. The party. Fifty years of marriage. Half the town coming – if any of them survived what was coming up on the other side of the mountain. The cake she'd baked that morning under the labouring air conditioner sat half decorated on the kitchen bench. *Happy 50th Wedding Anniversary* scrolled in silver across the top. The icing had spread, of course. Even her expert hand couldn't stop it running in this heat. It was disappointing, but there it was.

Keith was eyeing her from the chair.

'Don't worry, love. Dad saved this place in '39; I can too if I have to. Besides, the CFA boys will be here if we need 'em.'

Pat turned as a grubby four-wheel drive pulled into their driveway. The anxious face of their neighbour, James, leaned out of the window. Pat smiled, relieved to see someone new. Her nose wrinkled involuntarily. Even though she was standing four feet away, she could still smell the sweat on him. She'd never got used to the smell of the men in this town. There was an earthy stink about them, even after they'd showered, overpowering their Brut 33.

There was worry in James's eyes. He nodded to Pat and addressed Keith.

'Mate, things are getting pretty hairy. I've just been down the station and they're telling people it's time to get out.'

Keith stood and came to the top of the steps, his hands on his hips.
'That so? I haven't heard anything.'

Pat saw James tighten his lips. She could tell he was annoyed.

She looked back to Keith. He stood there, Superman like, staring a challenge at James, as if James was some kind of young fool without the brains to know real danger when he saw it. She liked James, he was a reliable sort of bloke. His presence now calmed her. She moved toward the car, placing her hand on the high bull bar. James glared back at Keith and persisted.

'You're hearing it now, Keith. The CFA's flat out trying to keep roads open. They said to head to the oval. It's the safest place. I can give you both a lift if you want.'

James glanced at Pat standing by the front of his car, holding the bull bar as if to keep him there. Pat looked up at the monstrous clouds rolling across the mountaintop. They were ugly and mean, like menacing trolls in a children's fairy tale. A growl of thunder reached them from the distance. She felt a flutter in her chest when she thought of what lay below those clouds. Keith hawked and spat in the dirt.

'No need. We'll be right.'

'Mate, I don't think you know what you're up against.'

Pat, hearing the urgency in James's voice, moved quickly toward her husband. She sensed Keith's hackles rise. That had done it. He was insulted and there'd be no changing his mind now.

'Keith, Darl, James is trying to help. Don't you think we should listen to him?'

Keith had pressed his lips together and straightened up to his full height, pushing his chest out toward James.

'I told you, we'll be right. The CFA'll be along if we get into strife. You'd want to be off, James. Leave the fire fighting to the men, ay?'

Keith turned and went inside the house. James was revving his engine, getting ready to go. Pat reached out toward the car, took a few hesitant steps toward it.

'Jimmy. Talk to him. Please?'

James glanced toward the screen door still swaying in Keith's wake and shook his head.

‘There’s no time, Pat. Sorry. You can hop in if you like.’

Pat’s shoulders sagged as she turned and looked at the house. Her husband. Her home. Her whole adult life: every moment, every memory, every part of what she had become, all in Keith’s stubborn, seventy-three-year-old hands.

‘C’mon, Pat, I’ve gotta go. There’s other people to warn.’

She took a step toward the car and smelled James again, smelled the smoke in the thick air. Dizziness overcame her and she staggered a little. She put her hand to her forehead. Opened her mouth. Closed it again. Waved James on. She couldn’t leave Keith alone. Not now.

She watched James reverse his car out of the driveway. He was shaking his head, his lips pressed in a silent curse. His tyres kicked up a shower of stones as he disappeared down the road toward town.

Pat glared at the Volvo before slowly climbing the steps and going into the house in search of Keith. She found him fiddling with batteries and the radio. The room was filled with a terrible silence. She realised the air conditioner was still. Everything was deathly quiet, except for the kitchen clock.

‘Why did you turn the air conditioner off?’

‘Damned power’s out,’ he mumbled.

Pat stared at the cake, the silver icing blurring in the building heat of the kitchen. The ‘50’ had become a fat blob. Spoiled. Too hot, too late, to save it now. What would people say when they saw it tomorrow? Tomorrow? Would there even be one if she stayed here with Keith tonight?

Pat wished she was somewhere far away with a big, wet ocean nearby. She thought about the cool southerlies of her youth. They could always be relied on. No matter how hot it got they’d show up, blasting away the sticky city heat, spinning clean threads of fresh air through the flyscreens. A city girl. That’s who she was. She’d never belonged up here among the wild gums, living in the shadow of a mountain that shut out the sun half the day. She didn’t want to be in this kitchen any more, with her ruined cake and mulish husband.

The car keys were sitting on the kitchen bench next to where Keith was working. Pat picked them up, felt their spiky weight in her hand. Usually they were cool to touch but today the metal was warm and tacky. Keith had stopped cursing the radio and was gazing at the contents of Pat’s hand. She pushed them over to him.

‘I’m scared Keith. I want to leave – please.’

She looked up at him, pleading with her eyes, hoping that some gentler part of him would give in to her, just this once. He picked up the keys and held them for a moment, then put them back in their place on the bench.

‘If I can get this damned battery in we might be able to hear what’s going on,’ he said.

Pat felt her age sinking down upon her, dragging her faith in Keith away from where it always had been. Fifty years. Fifty years of inland air drying her fine skin. Fifty years of second hand living, of making do in a house handed to them by Keith’s father. Fifty years of agreement. And he was willing to let it all end in one tiny word — *no.*

She left Keith fumbling with the radio and went to the bedroom to pick up her handbag. She walked quietly out of the front door, down the veranda steps, and over to the tap. She wet a handkerchief and tied it around her neck, making sure the hose was reconnected properly. He might need it.

Without a second glance she took to the road.
She had no idea where she was going or what she would do. Glowing ash floated around her and smoke stung her

eyes and lungs. She prayed a little, cried less. She forced one unsteady but determined foot in front of the other, her feet slipping and straining against the stiff vinyl. She wished she'd put on those damned boots, like Keith had told her to.

She listened out for Keith's voice, hoping she'd hear him calling her, but no sound came. She kept going, refusing to look back. It was all she could do if she was to save herself. The wind was picking up and changing direction. She felt it tug hard at her, twisted gusts of hot and cold pulling her away from the gravel and onto the road. She thought hard about the comfort of those southerly breezes, imagined the freshness of them, tied her resolve to the remembered smell of rain, until a vehicle pulled up beside her and a door flew open.

Pat climbed in beside the driver, barely acknowledging her. She was afraid if she broke the spell of what she was doing she might change her mind. She slammed the door behind her, knowing it was her last chance to turn and look at what she'd left behind. She forced her eyes straight ahead, avoiding the mirrors. She became aware of pain in her foot and bent down to rub a cluster of blisters grown fat on her swollen heel. The radio broadcast urgent warning after urgent warning, the presenter unable to contain her anxiety about what was happening beyond the safety of the studio walls.

The car gained speed, tyres rushing on scorched asphalt. Pat fiddled with the contents of her handbag and felt a pang of regret as she realised she'd forgotten something. A small but important thing. She bit her lip. The goodbye kiss, a ritual of every parting during their fifty years of marriage, but for today, and she couldn't go back now, it was too late. Tears filled Pat's eyes as she thought of Keith, alone on his veranda, the garden hose in his hand, staring out at the road and cursing her for her womanly stupidity. She wondered if he would survive without her parting kiss. So she did it in her mind. She closed her eyes and formed a gentle kiss on Keith's whiskery cheek and sent it rushing to him on the dust and ash of the cool change.

getting on with life

Françoise van der Plank

The first spots of ash came floating down like small white feathers, gracefully and lightly. You would have said snow, but of course no one was thinking of snow that day. Later the larger bits and pieces came floating down, some faster than others: whole eucalyptus leaves burnt totally black, beautiful in their starkness. Later still, small black twigs appeared, and fronds of what seemed to be ferns. Sara had to think hard to realize where the ferns could come from, but she decided they were probably from the moist gullies around Hall's Gap where there were semi-permanent creeks. All these things landed everywhere. On the ground, the house, the car, they drifted under the veranda, on the veranda, and even found their way inside the house through the odd gap. The ground was no longer just a clay colour. It turned into an artist's abstract dabbling of yellows, browns, white, grey and black, speckled and dotted, with random strong lines of organic silhouettes.

While Sara worked on raking more and more leaves and removing them from around the house, the air itself also turned into an artist's palette. The smoke was exceedingly thick at times and difficult to breathe. Its colour changed constantly, ranging from light grey, dark yellow and red to white, with all possible subtle nuances in between. Was it the sunlight way above, above the masses of smoke clouds, that caused these colour shifts? Were there perhaps clouds up there passing before the sun and making the air seem darker? It was impossible to tell. The whole day passed in an eerie smoke haze, with the sun sometimes an evil glaring red eye and sometimes just a vague fuzzy red object that was not especially brighter than any other object in vision.

She had read that bushfires come with a lot of noise, very scary, deafening noise. That meant the fire was not close yet: they didn't hear much at all. They could hear the wind every so often, a stronger faster airflow higher up in the sky, over their place, over the mountain. So that was the same as ever. Their place never suffered as much from the wind as other areas of the valley. You imagined, however, that this wind sounded more evil and more potentially dangerous. You couldn't see the fire. Maybe they never would, Sara thought. Hoped.

She took the two watering cans down the hill and watered the gum saplings they had planted the winter before. She had been so keen to 'fill in' the gaps between trees in the bush surrounding their house. It was a futile gesture: the plants were already scorched by the hot, dry air of the past few weeks. There was not much hope they would survive, let alone if the fire came through. And maybe it was not such a good place to have trees. Suddenly all the trees she loved so much seemed to be terribly close to the house. Paul raced around doing the fire safety activities they should have completed two months earlier. The children helped a little, but preferred to stay inside playing board games with each other, ignoring the disaster possibly bearing down on them.

The first day the fire threatened their area of the Grampians, it was a day of smoke and ash, but no flames. When Sara went down to the dam to check the pump and the hoses, she noticed that the surface of the water was covered in ash. It looked like a furry pelt on an animal, and when the water moved slightly with a breath of wind, you could swear it was a gigantic beast lying asleep, its fur rippling. Sara wondered whether any of the inhabitants of the dam would survive. The yabbies and fish had been poking their heads above the water the previous day. Whole regiments of yabbies lined the sandy shores of the dam, suffering perhaps from not enough oxygen left in the water.

Sara and Paul commented to each other on the strangeness of the situation, but she did not mention its beauty. Paul was tense. Sara doubted whether he would appreciate any comments on the artistic qualities of bushfire circumstances. He sought her support in preparing the house and grounds for ember attack and a possible fire front. And when they decided they could do no more that day, he sought distraction, so sat hunched over in front of the computer and worked on invoices, tax statements and money flow as if nothing unusual was happening at all. Sara rang a few family members who lived in the city and still had little idea of the situation, but found she was exaggerating the current circumstances to force some reaction: surprise or shock, any kind of emotion. She wanted them to share her sense of uncertainty and trepidation. She realized she wanted them to do the speculating for her. Unhappy with her own behaviour, she let off calling people, and decided not to send any more emails. After all, this was their own battle. They were the only ones who could do anything about it at this stage.

When they went outside after dark, it was hard to see anything. The air was thick with smoke; a torch beam showed the grey soup with even more ash and black, burned objects swirling around. Sara and Paul disagreed about the wind direction. The shock of the early evening, when flames were actually visible on the ridge and a fierce red glow lit up the mountain range, gradually subsided into an almost impatient waiting game: will the radio tell us we are under threat before the fire gets to us? Paul wanted to put the sprinkler system on immediately. Sara said it could take another ten hours so it was better to wait. They waited. The flames abated, the red glow diminished. The radio gave no news useful to them. They were disinclined to ring the information line. For a few hours they heard heavy machinery working to the east. Sara thought they must be digging out a control line just outside the Park boundary, where private land and dwellings began. That night they decided to take turns staying awake. Paul worked further on the computer during his shift. Sara read a book when it was her turn. She drank one glass of wine. She listened to the radio on the hour. She looked outside every so often and observed that the wind was strengthening and the smoke thickening. There was no red glow however, and no flames to be seen. No embers fell as far as she noticed.

She had never stayed up all night before and never been awake on guard like this in the middle of the night. That experience was new as was the entire experience of facing a bushfire. Sara wondered why she felt calm. She certainly didn't feel invincible, but she didn't think she would panic. She tried to remember their property the way it had looked when they moved in: the magnificent gum trees, the healthy understorey, the amazing grass trees. And all the animals! She hoped she would be able to hold on to those memories if the fire came through and nothing was recognisable any more.

The day the wind changed and turned into a gale in the other valley, they became more nervous. They followed the progress of the fire on the radio. They turned the sprinkler system on several times a day, cleared the verandas entirely of furniture and junk and had their fire gear ready by the door. Paul went to the community meeting and came home shaken and frightened. During the meeting reports had come in from the field: the fire front jumped control lines twice in that one hour. It was burning down the Asses Ears and had crossed Asses Ears Road.

The next day the danger became acute. The CFA drove past and discussed the situation. They couldn't predict or guarantee anything, but they knew the fire was very close and the winds stronger than desirable, in the wrong direction, and that the unfinished house was a vulnerable structure. They advised evacuation. So Paul and Sara decided to evacuate. The children spent an hour collecting their own valuable possessions, while Sara collected clothing, footwear, food and sleeping bags. Paul concentrated on disconnecting the main computer and getting all its parts into the car. When the CFA came tearing through a second time, with lights and sirens going at full blast, they told them to get out. So they did.

The days of living at the neighbour's 'safer' place down the road were a scrambled dream. The controlled back burns going out of control, the giant Elvis sky cranes sucking up water from the Smiths' dam and dumping their thousands of litres of water only a few hundred metres away from their home, all the fire fighting aircraft and the innumerable tankers and utes and bulldozers and graders, the noise, the smoke, the heat, the flames, the flies, the glow at night from one side of the valley right across to the far end of Asses Ears, the tense moments of listening to the ABC radio and hearing their own family name mentioned as a possible property loss, the succession of phone calls from family, neighbours and acquaintances, the mindless distraction of sport on the television, the nights of broken sleep, the cups of tea from morning till night till morning again: it all merged into one big impression that could have been one day or could have been ten days, but turned out to be three days because on Saturday they went back home.

The rain rinsed the ash off the roof, cleaned the gutters and piping and dampened much of the smouldering bush around the house. The children hadn't yet seen the destruction and devastation caused by the bulldozers, right through the property, nor had they seen the effects of the back burning at close proximity or visited the close edge of the actual fire front. 'Not as bad as we thought,' they said. 'Look, we can play with our Matchbox cars in these new piles of sand.' That helped Sara and Paul.

It took a few hours to reacclimatise to being back at home. Sara first wandered around aimlessly. Then she went down to where the gum saplings had been. The entire area seemed to have been flattened, just a mess of bare earth left by the grader. She bit back a sob and walked around, picking up the broken pieces of bamboo stakes she could find. Then she found it: one little tree on the edge of the area, still standing and apparently still alive. She ran up to the house and came back with the watering can. She watered the tree. It seemed to stand more strongly straight away. She bent down and touched its few leaves. When she stood up and looked around, she saw the toppled centuries-old red gums that had succumbed to the bulldozers and the blackened standing trees that had been burned and still smoked. But she also saw her little sapling.

Sara went back up to the house and started sweeping. The children were playing the piano. Paul wrote letters. When he lit the woodstove, Sara realized they were getting on with life again. So she made a pot of tea.

bushfire

Paul Hetherington

Tumultuous, for months
the aftermath of fire –
burnt stumps, spindles of trees,
ash rising on the slightest wind,
wafting, sinking
like particles of memory,
nights charred with recollection,
cries chasing conversations,
and incalescent weather
like 40 days of sunstroke
darkening the district.
The local store piled its verandah
with new goods,
stashed beer and milk
in its freezers. Its generator groaned
and, where the fire had caught it,
its west side leaned
into black-toothed grimace.
Someone picked up Jimmy's kite
twenty kilometres from the township.

Someone else wrote letters
to every politician in the district.
A teenage girl was seen
by three men walking
on the road out of town
although no girl lived there.
Rain came in drops like stones
clagging ash, banging roofs,
making molten dreams.

coming down to earth

Carmel Macdonald Grahame

In this layer of our domestic palimpsest,
I shop for towels, bathmats, etcetera,
Home stores offer a range of reincarnations,
and I can choose the colours, at least, in which
we go on being determined to start again.
Black is cool, modern, *in*, but disheartening.

The lost, last bathroom was green and white,
leafily lead-lit, well-supplied with the usual
certainties, subsiding now into an ash-bed
with all the details of our Saturday memories.
Only the margins of a house remain intact,
around burnt space embodying flatness.

Turns out comfort can be this precarious,
so my quest through unsettling displays
of life's minutiae is guided by necessity:
toothbrush-holders, towel racks, mirrors…
Such everyday rituals are far from trivial:
they concern familiarity, are love-specific.

Except, this hectic performance of bathrooms –
its cushiness, chrome trinketry, unrestrained
refurbishment, mad colour-chart geography,
massed paraphernalia for sluicing bodies –
fills me with misery, not a sense of renewal.
I am tethered to indecision by excess.

Then, bizarrely relocated, a dragonfly flits in
as if to lead my dwindling sense of possibility
into the spectrum – indigo, violet, black again –
its deft flight a pathway of suggestion,
even hesitating over green, like a question
about what we might not have to relinquish.

Oh, I know dragonflies are in fact insects
(*Odonata*, this one could be *Australestes Leda*)
and the encounter is actually meaningless,
but its unlikely appearance here reminds me

of erratic aerial dances, gauzy tandem flight,
nymphs, complicated water-hatchings, things ...

It holds the air in front of me, creaturely,
and steadily suspended as if to collaborate.
Close enough for me to see faceted light
thrilling on its silvery reticulated wings,
and to check for my own fractured reflection
in that mosaic gaze — we are eye to eye.

Mesmerised I almost whisper to it (lunatic),
ask who it used to be, or *Are you back*?
But it is no time for DIY mysticism. Resisting
thoughts of omens, I extend a hand, wishing
it would touch down on me, confer a blessing –
karma is in the air, it would be a good sign.

Naturally it leaves me to my lot, darting off,
flickering hints over monogrammed bathrobes,
a fleeting temptation from the limits of affinity
given their fluffy starlet pretensions, but
disturbing anyway to discover my initials
are missing from that embroidered alphabet.

Then, itself like a whim of aeronautic design,

the dragonfly inscribes a last swift puzzle of
trajectories on its bright incongruous airspace
and disappears into *Select Kitchens* –
another vein of loss in our former life's erasure.
So ends a delicate correspondence of being.

Except, I find myself settling on silvery greys
for colouring-in this layer of intimate emptiness:
lost everything, have to start all over again....
Even commonplace concessions to the future
might as well be lustrous; beginnings are
always new, always composed of fact-facing.

holyoake

Donna Mazza

Three concrete steps are left on the side of the hill. Once, they were painted green. They soak up the sun and make a place to sit amongst the remains. Sometimes on hillsides and in paddocks tall brick chimneys remain as a monument; but not here. The fire was too hot.

If it weren't for this place, there would be plenty of family heirlooms to squabble about. There was a collection of gramophones, some of them in pieces awaiting restoration, a hank of long blonde hair cut from a child of six and wrapped in a lace dress that once had lollipops sewn into the hem. There was a photo of Sid in a sailor suit in Saskatchewan

Sid and Jean drank lemonade in the Dwellingup shop. There was lemonade in the fridge at their own shop and he was getting a lift back to pick up the ute and the dog and they would wait on the oval with everyone else.

It was after 6 o'clock when they heard an explosion and looked down the gravel road. Holyoake roared. The heat of the bowsers exploding incinerated the bricks of the fireplace. Jean didn't believe it until she saw her burnt out fridge and all her beautiful china melted together and the huge trees gone. Completely gone.

The wind was strong, the fire coming their way. Jean's hair whipped against her cheeks in warm gusts which seemed to be blowing her down the gravel road and onto the bitumen and out of that fear where it was really happening after all. The postmistress was right when she told them to leave. They waited too long.

Sid thought about all this occasionally years later when he was holding his knife and fork in a lovely laminex kitchen. Sometime later he would tap the ash from his pipe on a cracked red step and plan to build a doll's house but in January 1961 he pulled up his trousers, tightened his braces and grasped the steering wheel of his green Austin thinking he would rather stay on the oval in Dwellingup with everyone else. Jean wanted to get out. He was afraid and nobody was leaving with them down the smoky road in the dark. He thought of his girl Jean, smiling in her war-time shoes by a water tank, her legs so small and definite. He saw the panic wriggling wildly in her blue eyes and drove into the smoke. They were the last car to leave Dwellingup that night.

She could not stop screaming and screaming at the windscreen nightmare. Trees were blazing all around. Engines and machines tried to extinguish the forest but the roar of the fire was louder and the wind and flames chased them down the road with furious crackling. Sid squinted in the smoke and could barely see to guide the green Austin as fast as it could go and branches fell and burnt behind and all around and flames raged either side down that long descending road. Even through the smoke she could smell Sid's tobacco. Her face grew red and blistering from the heat inside the car. She listened to the falling trees, the crackling and screaming all around. Eyes closed; hoping him into the creek, his howl echoing through silent, smoky Holyoake.

The Daily News read:

> Raw-eyed, blackened and weary people told of the worst night of terror in WA history as the inferno roared on the

town. People fled for their lives leaving everything behind as hurricane force wind turned the town into an inferno.

The next morning, Margaret stared into her red and peeling face, still warm and numb and soaking in Skin Repair in the round mirror on Aunty Iris's pink bathroom wall. Her heart hoped for three days and on the fourth day Sid drove them back home.

Ransackers had already combed the debris, kicking the hot metal and glass, finding an axe head, blistering their fingertips. The ground was still hot and Jean found her silver thimble, black with soot. Margaret ran to the creek. He wasn't there and her heart sank and she screamed when they found him all curled up and dead and shaped like a dog but just a pile of ashes all safe and sound under Jean's burnt out iron bed where he would hide when he was really scared. All she could smell was ash; everywhere was ash.

Now the back steps have soaked up the sun, become a warm place to sit. Runners of wisteria search for something to climb. We dig up a piece and plant it at home. And she still can't talk about it without crying.

the minutiae of homes lost

Heidi Trudinger

Synopsis

These photographs are of objects found amid the rubble of homes lost in the Black Saturday bush-fires in Victoria, 2009. For many people, these small relics are the only objects that survived the fires. To find such objects was meaningful and they were kept, becoming significant as the destroyed homes and contents were hauled into trucks and taken away.

These 'little things' are held dear as mementos of the past, a time now commonly termed by us all as 'before the fires.' Fragments of stories and memories, they hold a new place our lives as we rebuild the 'stuff' that surround us and reflect us in our new homes.

The substances that survive fire — being metal, glass and ceramic — are the ones that use intense heat in their manufacture. These often strange and beautiful objects have been transformed once more by fire, and are — like the many individuals affected by this natural disaster — forever changed but still recognisable.

A grandmother's perfume bottle

A stolen marble, a treasured bottle

The Christmas tea cups

raining blood and money: remembering the triangle shirtwaist fire

Cassandra Atherton

'I learned a new sound -- a more horrible sound than description can picture. It was the thud of a speeding, living body on a stone sidewalk. Thud-dead, thud-dead, thud-dead, thud-dead.' William G. Shepherd, 'Eyewitness at The Triangle', Milwaukee Journal, *27th March, 1911.*

A girl jumps from the ninth floor of the Asch building. People on the sidewalk are screaming for her not to jump. But she has to jump. As she stands on the ledge, her back against the open window, the fire is burning the clothes off her back. She has her head bent forward so her hair doesn't catch alight as she waves a handkerchief at the crowd. The windows on the floor beneath her start to explode. Tongues of flame lick at her feet. So she jumps. It's a definite jump, as she bends her knees before she leaps over the edge. It's not a graceful jump. Her arms begin to flail as she struggles to stay upright. There are gasps from the crowd, a few screams. Some people turn away. Others are transfixed, watching her as she falls. Suddenly, her dress catches on a hook jutting out of wall below and she is suspended in the air, mid-fall. But the ladders still can't reach her and so it is just a cruel pause in her inevitable death. She hangs there like a ragdoll until her dress burns itself free from her body and she resumes her fall. She lands on the pavement on the westward side of New York University building. Thud-dead.

Three girls clamber onto the same window-sill from where the first girl jumped. They hold hands. They are standing in descending order of height. The tallest one turns to the other two. She says, 'One, two, three,' as they all bend their knees at the same time and jump over the edge, the two smallest staring into the tallest one's eyes. They try to keep hold of one another's hands, but they fall at different speeds. They hit the pavement in descending order of height. Thud-dead. Thud-dead. Thud-dead.

Groups of girls edge along the window-sill. One group waits for the firemen to confidently spread their nets before they jump. They are on target as they fall, closing in on the middle of the net. Perhaps they will hit the net and spring up, like an acrobat. But the nets are torn from the firemen's hands with the weight of the falling girls. The men try to signal to the girls to jump one at a time, but they cling to one another for comfort and come crashing down in threes and fours. The girls grouped on the ledge watch their friends strike the pavement. Perhaps they can hear them in their final moments. Perhaps they imagine they can hear them take their final breath. Or do they exhale with that final thud-dead?

When the firemen raise their ladders they only reach the sixth floor and the water shooting from the hoses only wets the seventh. The hose wagon, when it arrives, takes a while to be manoeuvered into position. Initially it has to avoid crushing the pile of already mounting bodies. Three girls make a dive for the top rung of the ladder. All three miss and come tumbling down, head first. Their beautiful faces smash against the sidewalk. One of the girls hurtles into a street-light before her broken body lands on a pile of others beneath her. A muted thud-dead.

It looks as if rags are being tossed from the building. It doesn't take long to realise that these fabric remnants and bolts of cloth, are in fact young immigrant workers throwing themselves out of the windows to escape the fire.

A policeman and a fireman stretch out a horse's blanket and signal for one of the girls on the ledge to jump. She does but the blanket is rent in two with the weight of her body and she falls to her death, like all the others. Rip. Thud-dead.

Three men bravely make a human chain from one of the windows on the eighth floor to a window below, away from the flames. They balance precariously; a human ladder stretching to safety. A few women are able to climb across their backs to safety. Clutching at their clothes, sliding down the length of their bodies, it seems to be working. Until the men eventually lose their balance and tumble to the ground. They grapple and grab at the building as they fall. But they are falling too fast to get a hold of anything at all. In the end, they crash through the vault lights on the pavement into the basement and land face down. Another ten thud-deads and then the sound of water from the hoses rushing in on top of the bodies. More bodies land in the basement. The water douses the flames on the girls' skirts and bodices and washes away the blood, but it laps against the walls, thick with charred pieces of cloth, hair, skin and bones.

Another girl stands on the ledge. She throws her purse, hat and coat down first, as if she will retrieve them later, and then she jumps. She, too, lands in the basement, on top of all the others. And more will land on top of her. The basement echoes a watery series of thud-deads.

A man appears at one of the windows. Behind his head is a halo of fire. He looks out in desperation. The choice is clear: be burnt alive or jump. He disappears for an instant only to return with a woman. He grabs her by the waist and lifts her out through the window. He doesn't place her on the window-sill, instead, he positions her so that her legs dangle over the ledge. She looks back at him and he drops her over the edge. She falls, flailing and kicking until she crumples on the pavement. Thud-dead. The man appears with a second woman. She kisses him on the forehead before he drops her from the ninth floor. She lands near the first girl, a pile of clothes and broken bones. Thud-dead. He returns with a third girl. He appears calm as he edges her out of the window. She hangs onto his arms for a second until she, like the two before her, are hurtling through space. Her skirt and petticoats billow around her; a sky dancer. Until, thud-dead. A trio of lifeless bodies on the sidewalk. The man returns, but something is different this time. The flames are closer but he doesn't want to let this girl go. His arms encircle her waist. She turns to him for strength. He looks at her, for the last time, smoothes back her hair and kisses her. There is tenderness and desperation in their embrace. He lets her go. She falls from her Capulet balcony but there is no-one to catch her. Before she lands he springs onto window ledge. He jumps and his trouser legs fill with air. He is wearing tan coloured shoes. He has a hat on his head. His fiancé lands before him but he does land next to her. Their arms overlap; they look as if they are reaching for one another, even in death. The small diamond on her ring finger glints in the flames of the fire. She never knew the emotion of a white wedding dress or the strong arms of her husband in bed. Thud-dead. Thud-dead.

Doctors and interns make their way to each of the broken bodies. One girl is still burning. She looks like a candle as her hair is aflame. The doctor rips the remnants of her burning clothes from her body and puts out her flaming hair. Her limbs are still moving. She is given a painkiller and placed on a stretcher and taken to the hospital. She dies before she gets there. A second girl is placed on a stretcher. Her dress is covered in blood and her head is split open. She is barely alive. An onlooker says she is 'ninety nine percent dead.' She, too, dies only moments later. One hundred percent dead. They tag the bodies and cover them with tarpaulins.

Fifty-four men and women jump from the 8th, 9th and 10th floors that day. Two of the girls are found alive, hours after

they fall, covered by other bodies. But they die, too. No-one survives that jump. Every thud results in a death.
Two men are still operating the elevators in the building. They are running their elevators up and down the building, cramming as many singed and burning women into the lift as they can. Every time they open the doors, women flood into the lift. They have to leave dozens behind. They move swiftly past the flames until the fire enters the elevator shaft and the lifts no longer function. It is partly because the metal is twisted by the fire but also because more than twenty women have jumped to their deaths and landed on the roof of the descending elevator. The weight of their bodies pushes the elevator down to the basement where it remains. It rains blood and money in the lift. The dead girls' coin purses open and their week's wages spill out. How many blouses did they have to make for that money; how many shirtwaists did they have to sew for $6.00 a week; how many plans did they have for the weekend – the Nickelodeon, Coney Island, time with their families?

Firemen rush up the stairs. The Asch building is fireproof on the outside but is a tinderbox on the inside. Nineteen bodies are melted against the locked door on the ninth floor. They try to peel the bodies off, layer by layer, but it is hard to tell where one body ends and the next begins. The dark secret at the heart of the Triangle Shirtwaist Company is Bluebeard's locked room. Locked doors kept the workers from taking unauthorised breaks. Locked doors kept the workers from stealing. Locked doors kept the workers from escaping the fire. They are sealed in with their twisted sewing machines and the inferno. Groups of bodies huddle together like Pompeii's victims. Frozen in their final moments. Arms linked, they shield their melted faces from the flames. They die in these pow-wows; Jewish, Italian and German immigrant workers, dying in one another's arms.

Orange gives way to smoking black. Out of the same gaping windows through which dozens of men and women jumped to their deaths, firemen begin to lower the charred bodies of those entombed in the building, two and three at a time. Policemen use their horses' blankets and lay the corpses and burnt body parts out along Greene Street. A ghostly procession stretches down the street. Soon there are no blankets left and multiple bodies and burnt body parts share the one blanket. The corpses are waxen and black. Clothes are reduced to ashes, burnt deep into flesh. Some of the bodies are naked and their limbs have burnt away, leaving charcoal stumps. Some still have some flesh clinging to their bones, but they are unrecognisable. Many, only a few hours ago, had sat side by side at sewing machines and now they lie side by side in death. Dozens of engagement rings are scattered in the remains on the eighth and ninth floors. Eternal promises in those tiny bands of gold and coloured gems are swept into shoeboxes with other personal belongings and the scorched remnants of material. Some families will have to identify their daughters from these mini-coffins. For some families there is no body to bury; just ash. Ashes to ashes and dust to dust.

The bodies, body parts and belongings are taken to Bellevue Morgue. They are put into coffins, the lids left off, ready for families to identify their children. Some are so disfigured that they have to be identified by personal jewellery items and even the buckles on their shoes. As they are identified, the lids are nailed down, ready for burial. There are so many bodies that they spill out onto the tin-roofed Charities pier, adjacent to the morgue. There are not enough coffins and more have to be ordered from Blackwell's Island.

146 people died in 18 minutes in the Triangle Shirtwaist fire. Someone probably threw a cigarette butt into the scrap bin, it ignited the fire and 129 women and 17 men asphyxiate, burn to death or die of internal injuries. In time, their families will learn that their children's lives are only worth $75 a piece. The owners, Harris and Blanck are acquitted of locking the

doors; a civil suit brought by twenty-three families results in the sum of 75 silver pieces for each of their daughter's lives.

It rains on the day of the public funeral procession. The final six unidentified bodies are buried at the Cemetery of the Evergreens in Brooklyn. The black umbrellas of the mourners stand out against the grey sky. More than 120,000 march, while 230,000 more gather in churches, synagogues and watch as the slow procession makes it way through the streets of the Lower East Side. There is nothing but the noise of the raindrops falling on the pavement; a reminder of the bodies hitting the pavement to escape the fire, only eleven days earlier. No-one speaks.

The International Ladies' Garment Workers' Union and the Women's Trade Union League break the silence with their renewed fights for better working conditions and protective legislation. This time their words are substantiated with photographs in the newspaper of the bodies lining the pavement beneath the Asch building and tortured black corpses melted onto the locked door on the ninth floor. Union ranks swelled from 30,000 in 1909 to 250,000 in 1913. Now, no doors are to be locked during working hours, sprinkler systems must be installed if a company employs more than 25 people above the ground floor, and fire drills are mandatory for buildings lacking sprinkler systems.

Today, students look out through the same windows on the ninth floor where so many jumped to their deaths, a century ago. The Asch building is now the Brown Building of Science and belongs to New York University. The students, like the immigrant workers before them, have dreams about working hard, playing by the rules and getting ahead. But the smoking chimneys they can see from this vantage point, indicating the sweatshops that are still operating all over New York , belie this American Dream.

no surrender

Dorothy Simmons

The needle in the old woman's hand stops moving: firelight glints in dilated eyes.

...flames leaping high, higher; the straw man at the top of the pyre explodes, torching the night sky. Sparks shoot through the air like gems, like stars: holding out the skirt of her best blue dress to wonder at the brightness of the one that chose her, raising her eyes to Pat's ashen face...plunged choking and thrashing into a horse trough, soaked and sodden, chilled to the bone...

It was branded into her memory, deeper than any burn: that locked eye terror, her brother's fierce hands thrusting her under water, the frenetic bubbles: the ecstasy of his cold wet arms crushing her to his chest...

The bonfires were in memory of the Siege of Derry. Derry, never Londonderry, even if the Protestants did run the place. The scarecrow at the top of the biggest fires was Lundy, who'd tried to give the city back to James the Second and got murdered for his trouble. The king laid siege to the city. But the Prods won, said Patrick. Yes, said her Da, they won. James might have been the rightful Catholic king, but that didn't stop him being as thick as two short planks. He went and lost the throne to that bigwig Dutchman: William of Orange.

The Prods of Derry were all for Orange Billy. Her Da pointed at the big letters daubed on the walls: 'No Surrender'. He said they'd eaten rats and dead dogs sooner than give in. Ignorant bastards: but they had guts, you had to give them that. Which was the whole point, wasn't it? Her Da put his hand on Patrick's shoulder.

'They'll never give an inch, son. Not one inch.'

Her big brother's arm tightened around her. 'Well, we won't surrender either. Will we, Nell?'

She'd told Ned and Maggie that story straight after Red's funeral. The next day, in the kitchen, she'd heard Ned retelling it to Jim and Dan. Talking about her like she wasn't his mother at all, like she was somebody entirely different. And so she was, so she had been: pretty little Nell in her blue dress… Nell Quinn. Not Ellen Kelly. Not the notorious Ellen Kelly.

A log drops in the fireplace, startling her back to here, to now: to the darkness outside, her mending basket on the floor, Jim's empty chair opposite. Wouldn't be back till tomorrow. And late, probably. She'll have to cope with that boyo on her own. Ah well, won't be the first time. With a sigh, she lifts the quilt on her knees, takes the next stitch. Stitch after stitch after stitch after stitch.

Law after law after law after law: books of them, courtrooms of them. Laws against selling grog, laws against assault, against robbery, against abusive language. But what about laws against robbing the words out of folk's mouths? Where were they? Or putting words into folks' mouths, making things happen that never ever did, what about laws against changing the story entirely? Changing a brand was nothing to that.

Cookson, he said his name was. From *The Sun*...hah, standing there at her door in the pouring rain. Drowned rat...but a rat just the same. A reporter. A journalist. A liar.

Lies, lies, lies! The hide of the man, warming his hands at her fire, spouting such a lot of...slander, that's what it was, bloody slander. That Dan and Steve had got away, that the two of them were running around South Africa alive and well. As if anybody could have got out of that inferno. As if her own son wouldn't have come straight to her, or let her know, as if her Danny would ever have abandoned his own mother. As if all that was left of him and poor Steve wasn't a couple of miles down the road, six feet under. As if...Jesus wept. She shook her head. The look on the man's face when she told him who she was!

She squints into the eye of her needle; she can still thread a needle, though she's not as quick any more. Her eyesight's always been good. Right back to that long ago last day when her Da took the horse and cart and drove them all the way up to the Giant's Causeway, right up to the topmost end of Ireland: *farewell to old Ireland forever*...she was the one who spotted the old woman among the rocks, for all the world like a rock herself, set down there huddled up in her black shawl.

‘Is she a witch, Da, is she a witch?’
‘Not at all, just a poor oul’ soul trying to earn a penny or two. That’s what they call the Wishing Well; cross her palm with silver and she’ll tell you your fortune.’

He winked at Patrick.

‘Think she’s heard of Australia?’
‘Can we, Da? Can we? Cross her palm...’
‘ Aye, why not. Why the hell not, eh? Last day on the oul’ sod...’

The old woman had a jug beside her and it had poteen in it; her Da bought some for himself and Ma and for Patrick. The rest of them were supposed to make do with water from the well, but she sweet-talked Pat into giving her a sip. The hard fast burn of it made her choke and her eyes water; but then the clouds lifted and the sun shone through like a blessing. The old woman made them all stand in a circle, cross their fingers and close their eyes all at the same time; then count one two, three...make a wish...

When she opened her eyes, the old woman was looking straight at her, her eyes two glinty eggs in a nest of wrinkles, her smile wide and toothless. She knows, Ellen thought. She knows mine’s different. So when the others told her Da what they had wished, she would not, not even when he promised her a pony of her own as soon as they got settled in Australia. Because she knew that sure as she told anybody, her wish wouldn't come true.

More than ever, now, a lifetime away, her own face a nest of wrinkles, she wants that wish to come true. But not for herself any more. For the only one she ever did tell. She wants it to be his story that people would tell after he was gone.

Thank God her Da never lived to see it. For him, Ned would always be the pick of the bunch, the only one in the same league as his own Patrick. Ellen winced. Pat was 25 when he drowned. So was Ned when they hung him.

What if she had had the Sight herself? Would it have made any difference ?

Her eyes flick from quilt to flames to quilt. Not a chance. She jabs her needle in fiercely. The same stitches, over and over and over and over. Like the memories stitched over and over in her head.

She still jumps at the knock of a door. A train whistle still shrieks her back twenty years: prison gates clanging behind her, stepping onto the train from Melbourne to Glenrowan: three years done, a lifetime to do.

There was an old man called Michael Finnigan, he grew fat and then grew thin again; then he died and had to begin again, poor old Michael Finnigan, begin again...

There were always the songs. Evenings at the old Eleven Mile before Jim moved her out to Greta West, evenings with Tom and Maggie and Jim and Kate, even Wild Wright, mad bugger that he was, when they could still get up a bit of a song and dance: years ago now. There was neither the heart nor the strength for it any more. The only singing she does now is to send the grandchildren to sleep.

Minding and mending. Stitching time.

Ned minding his letters. Him and Joe minding together, making up letters, trying to mend what was already beyond mending. What do you think, will we call it a 'colonial stratagem'? We will, that's the very word. And 'fair warning': we will give them fair warning, will we not? Which is more than they ever gave us. Rub it in, make them see the injustice. 'I am a widow's son outlawed.' And so he was.

Maggie said he was still writing his letters in gaol. Nothing else to do, I suppose. Scraps of paper, hooks of words cast into the stream, fishing for yesterday or the day before. Trying to catch something worth keeping.

In the Beginning was the Word; and at the end. Keeping your word.

Maggie memorised bits and pieces he told her, even wrote some of them down. God knows what happened to them. She would have liked to try to read those letters. It would be slow work, but she would have remembered, would have worked it out, however long it took...stitch by word, word by stitch.

*D'you mind the time...*flat on her back in that narrow bed, hands crossed over her chest, eyes open on the dark, remembering times long gone: sitting herself down by Ned, her finger following his down the rows of print, across and back, across and back, till she got tired. Till it got too hard to keep the lines separate, or the times, or the places: to remember what had been done and what had been dreamt, what had been said and what had only been thought. More and more, it didn't seem to matter much. Because the ending never changed.

She'd trained herself to keep her eyes shut, to make it last, put off for as long as possible the pale, sickly light of day drizzling in through the bars. Sometimes, she pressed her fists into her eyes and held them there. When she took them away, the cell walls tilted and curved, landscapes loomed through cold stone and voices sang out or whispered in her ear. The here and the now cancelled each other and just for a little while the world came alive again...

Red's beard, red and ticklish on her breast: firelight flickering over children's faces of a nighttime: the squawk of the peacock at Glenmore: shut your eyes, shut your eyes, hold on to it, that world of the high, bright air. Tir na n-og, her mother used to call it. 'The land of the young.' Ned. Dan. Kate. Maggie.

In Tir na n-og people never died, never grew old, just like her children would never grow old. Their smooth faces drifted in and out of her dreams, their voices so clear you'd swear they were only next-door...Maggie. Kate. Ned. Dan. Talking to her, reminding her, reviving her. Except for Dan. In her dreams, Dan never said a word. Which she didn't understand. Her Danny who never used to shut up, who whistled as he shoveled, who was forever skiting to her about what he and the Mob were up to, or about some girl he fancied, or wanting to know if she thought he'd grown. It was like he was in one of his sulks...

Ellen's needle stops again. Flames flicker and glow. No, not a sulk. Of course. All these years, why hadn't she seen sooner? Of them all, Dan was the talker; and talk about what, tell her what, what was the thing he never got to tell anyone about? The fire: the fire, of course. Glenrowan inn, that bitter blaze, that hellfire: ashes to ashes. What it was like for him and Steve, in there at the end of the world, in there knowing that everything was spoiled...

A spark leaps and dies.

It wasn't the fear, it wasn't the panic, it wasn't even the sight of the flames stabbing through the smoke that kept him quiet; it was her. Her and her temper, her blistering tongue, her red rages. That day, that day Red finally died: the state she'd been in that day, mad, raging, striding up and down... she'd made each one of them lay a hand on their dead father's body. She'd made each one of them swear by Almighty God that they would never do what their father had done. Never give up on themselves, never give in to the bastard traps or squatters or prison walls or the bloody bottle. No surrender, she said, don't any one of you dare bloody surrender the way he did. Because if you do, I tell you, it's as good as taking your own life and that is a mortal bloody sin. It's the sin God won't forgive you, not ever, not for all eternity, and no more will I. Kill yourself and it's me you're killing, your own mother.

They all swore. They all hugged each other. Seeing them with their arms around each other, their bent heads close, calmed her. That was it, that was the right thing to do. Bind them together as a family. Kellys, every one. Poor Red, poor pissweak Red: he'd have wanted her to do it too. God help him, he knew what that was like, turning into something you couldn't look at in a mirror. Something she couldn't look at either, something she was ashamed of. Though she'd never said that out loud, swear to God, she'd never said that out loud; yet somehow Danny must have known, must have remembered as his world came crashing down round him...

The flames flicker and glow. She leans forward and watches.

The inn was ablaze; the acrid stink and glare of it everywhere. Beams were cracking, glass exploding. Dan and Steve stood staring down at Joe, spread-eagled on the floor, but they were not looking at the dark red stain around his groin. They were looking at his face, his expressionless, gloriously, enviably indifferent face. His freedom.

They met each other's eyes. Without a word, Dan went and got their hats from where they'd tossed them on the bar. They put them on and tilted them, just so. Adjusted the chinstraps under their noses. Did up their top buttons, raised one leg after the other to polish their boots on the backs of their trousers. Gave each other the Greta Mob salute. Pulled out their pistols. Walked away from each other, turned, squared their shoulders, stood at ease. With their free hands, they crossed themselves. One long shuddery breath and Dan started the count down, her Danny. Three...lift arm, aim...two...locked into each other's eyes...

Crash! Crash!

The flames leapt and lunged, licking like famished tongues.

She blinks away the tears. So it was. Beyond certain. All the police got in the end was a couple of bodies, same as all they got was Ned's body. No surrender. No bloody surrender. Nothing for her to forgive, not now, not ever.

Danny, Danny. If only she'd seen it sooner, if only she could have told Maggie. It would have eased the girl, helped her sleep of a night instead of working herself to a standstill. Taking it out of her own hide, that was the way Maggie coped. She knew, because it was the same way she coped herself. And her mother before her.

Evenings at Eleven Mile: Maggie set by the hearth, latest baby at her breast, the fire lighting her face. Talking about the children, or Tom, or what needed doing about the place. Maggie's eyes resting on the old hat hung on the wall, her voice slowing.

'Thought he was that flash, him in his hat and the strap under his nose, didn't he? Leader of the Mob.'

Ellen nodded. 'It was his idea, you know. He told me. The strap under the nose.'

'I know.'

'I told him it was daft looking. He told me I was daft looking, only difference was, I couldn't help it.'

They laughed.

The funny things, the silly little things, they were all Maggie would ever talk about. Out loud. As if the funny things could block out the charred stumps, the legless, faceless, blistered stumps of boys: only boys. Talking around and around the nightmare; it had been the death of her daughter; she knew it had. Two trapped and tortured animals, the pain and the terror, she had never been able to get past that. But it wasn't like that, she knows that now. The relief of it...in the light of the fire, the old woman's face glistens; the line of her lips softens. She will think of her daughter before she goes to sleep, she will raise her. Tell her they sprang the trap. No surrender.

The fire is getting low; it's late. Hardly worth putting on another log. Ellen bends forward: that little one will do. Keep yourself warm, Maggie used to say. Mind you keep yourself warm, Ma. She stretches out her hands to the flames; she can almost see through them, the skin stretched around the thick knots of vein, the knobby fingers, the brown spots. She could do with Maggie now. Maggie was like Ned, Maggie could always think of a stratagem.

'Have you heard the latest? That Dan and Steve bolted? What'll we do, Ma?'

'Stick to our story, stick to Ned's story. Same as we've always done.'

'But this is nothing to do with Ned's story. That journalist says

there's no actual proof those bodies were theirs. Dear God, who the hell else's could they be? Never mind that you're his mother. Is that not proof enough for anyone? A mother's word?'

'When have they ever taken my word for anything? No, it'll have to be something else. Something that Dan had on him... something I can show that boyo when he comes sniffing around tomorrow...'

Ellen folds her quilt, tucks it carefully into the basket. She reaches into her apron pocket and takes out a scorched and blackened twist of metal. It is a hoof pick. She turns it in her hand: her oldest son holding up Mirth's foreleg, scraping out the hoof; the mare turning her head, nudging Ned's back. His hand reaching out to where Dan was pincering the redgold horseshoe up off the anvil, dipping it to hiss for a moment in the bucket, passing it to his brother...Ellen picks up her sharp scissors and resumes scraping at the initials etched into the scorched metal. D K; they glint in the firelight. Jesus wept: the one time he matched it with his brother and they want to take it away from him. Well, damned if they will. Damned if they will.

at glendalough monastery

(County Wicklow, Ireland)

Judy Johnson

'time is the fire in which we burn'
Delmore Schwartz

What the Normans left standing
flames licked in 1160.

There's no roof
above the domed entrance

where sky strains pines
through the gap.

The remaining gravestones
			are grey teeth

poking through
a winding-sheet of mist.

Once, a pilgrimage to Rome
equalled seven to Glendalough

But if there's residue
			of all that's happened here

			it does not settle as holiness
									nor peace:

but something more obdurate.
			Adamantine

as the local stone, ground down
to its calciums.

Glendalough makes no distinction
between the ash of now
			and the sixth century

when the Papacy
seasoned wood

for the first ever witch burning
in nearby Kilkenny.

And the Irish found a way
to transfigure

the all consuming Word
of the Christian book

into the less flammable vellum
of their illustrated faith.

Above prayer rock,
blackbirds and wind

kindle the space between
heaven
and earth.

I'll take your picture
the guide says
reaching for my camera.

As I pose in front
of the circular
blackened tower,
to the left of a Celtic cross,

something *is* taken from me
and not returned.

My after-image perhaps
still there in Glendalough.

What else would explain
the likeness I am left with

in the final picture?

Diminished, somehow. Blending into
the wintering filter.

It's only the ruined monuments around me
that have passed

through the fires of time,
that seem real.

the great kiln

In the voice of The Yellow Emperor
— 27th Century BCE, China

Michelle Leber

In my ninetieth year —
observing the minister
of tripods at his furnace,
I applaud flames
excelling in their duty
of baked vessels.

Moths fly out of my whiskers
to settle on the hearth, it is then
I grasp the notion that all life
is slanted towards the sun.

How on these shaky legs
does a man at his height concede to
darkness over pastures?
When height is fleeting?
Predestined visions

are weary geese, shadowy forms.
Isn't it enough that we carry
fear as useless fuel?

Surrender with each step
toward the fire. *Am I a moth?*
Lose attachment, bitterness, control —
proceed as if things were done

by no one.

isaac's land is burning

Miranda Aitken

You pack
your car full
of unusual
combinations
ten t-shirts
no underwear
leave
baby photos
by the back door
two men
to face a fire

You flee
the house
the hill
the smoke
the ash
the heat
the roar
Safety is
anxious
boredom
Safety is
time ticking
like a child's
icecream in
melting sun
while on the hill
smoke clouds
build and climb

into the sky
Celluloid cinders
float on
into town
and a river
receives
history's
scattered
ashes
New green
heals but
still it feels like
only yesterday
you needed
to flee

firestorm

Jo Gardiner

March 1945, Tokyo

Each night I sit upon the turning world in a garden cultivated by neglect. I watch the moon make shadows fall and wait for the mountain crow to deliver its letter, pour darkness from its throat.

Far away, faint charcoal lines of rain serrate Mount Fuji's dark skin. Above it, stars wheel like flocks of silver-winged birds. A frost is coming. I leave the garden and slip into the house before day breaks open. Under my threadbare goose-down quilt, I follow my English language lessons so that I may have an occupation of my own when peace comes, as Father wished. That will give me independence, and together we will rebuild our lives after this war.

I long for Father's return from Burma where he went with the army years ago. No word of him has come. As much as I yearn to see him again, I dread telling him that last year my mother was killed in the department store bombing. She wanted the ribbons they sold there and was dithering, reluctant to go, thinking Father might return while she was out shopping. I wanted to read in peace and said, For goodness sake, Mother, if you are going, just go!

The house is so quiet now.

Soon, beneath skeins of wild geese calling, I doze off. But even as I sleep, I am waiting in a pond of darkness. And just when I think it will always be dark, just when I think it will never reappear, light comes flickering through the birch trees.

Is it the night watchman's midnight call that wakes me?

I turn my face into the pillow and groan, so weary of this war, the actions of the Emperor. I smell smoke. I sit up, abruptly awake. For a moment, I believe Father is smoking Peace cigarettes in the next room. Then I hear high-pitched sirens. Do they foretell the vengeance of heaven, the end of empire?

Bi-nijuku's here, a voice shrieks. Hana, get up. Come to the shelter.

My neighbour, Mr Kyuku, appears at the door. His mouth is twisted half open, his face pale from lack of sleep, eyes glazed in a way that has become more usual for all of us since the raids.

Hana! he screams when I don't move.

Mr Kyuku! I'm coming, I call, scramble from the bed, pull on a jacket, catch up my emergency satchel and rush from the room into the freezing night. Flickering overhead are our tiny planes, flashes of searchlight beams. Another raid. A shudder runs through me. Mr Kyuku's right. I recognise the duller, lower rumble of the gods of calamity, approaching American bombers, huge, heavy B29s resolutely labouring under their loads. In my bones I feel their dull vibrations.

As neighbours hurry out of their houses, sirens wail on and on, broken by whistling and whizzing. I can see planes stacked up at different altitudes. The sky is the battleground. The air is falling. The clouds know that X marks the spot, that between midnight and dawn, hell comes to earth.

My breath comes faster. It's so dark without the moon but I can see long-winged silver planes like comets, a merciless armada in loose formation. The clouds have abandoned us, left us unprotected from these swollen, bloated bombers.

Light, light, someone has fallen here, a voice calls out, Get a light.

And immediately, as in the times of great fortune, prayers are answered and light comes: like a swarm of fireflies released from their cage, more bombs illuminate the night.

I rush across the garden and through the birch trees. The air's congested, cluttered, the sky stippled with planes. Dread sucks at me. I register the different nature of this night's violence: the very stars are on fire. Bombs of jellied-gasoline spread fire on a sour wind, set the air alight, torch it. Trees twist wildly, trying to flee.

Mr Kyuku waits for me at the gate.

This is bad, Hana. He grasps my satchel and slings it over his shoulder. We have to get to the shelter now.

Together we join the crowd jogging down our lane. Close above my head disoriented winter wrens swim through air clotted with embers and their small cries. I count the beats between blasts, the way you do between thunder and lightning. Spewing fire, the sky's a red wound. This time it's a maelstrom, a deluge of fire; the whole world spasms in a grotesque flowering, an ugly blossoming of flame.

I gasp, can't breathe. Others pant alongside me. I run as fast as I can, but violent strokes of fire stalk air, consume it, close it down. What's left broils with heat, with smoke and ash.

The river, I gasp. We haven't got time to get to the shelter.

A fine rain of fire falls on our heads. The air crackles and warps. From behind me come low moans of fear. Another sound rides above it: wind chimes hanging from the eaves of a house ring crazily, intone a weird tune. Fresh blasts come like slow-flung red hair. Ahead of us, a woman presses a package to her chest. She doesn't seem to know the baby on her back's ablaze.

Please help me, begs a man as he grabs my arm.

With open palms I slap at the fire on his jacket, his hair. Suddenly he sees the canal and runs off towards it. From the burning Kototoi Bridge, the flaming man dives into the canal.

I weave away between houses, along alleys, my skin lacquered with sweat as the human tide carries us towards the Sumida River. The sky haemorrhages fire. No one speaks now. Cascades of sparks scatter in the night before a wall of wind.

A pale cat, its fur alight, races across our path and trips me in its flight. It yowls as I stumble. My stride lengthens as I struggle to remain upright. I lose equilibrium. As I go down, I watch Mr Kyuku being swept up in the current of human beings pouring down the street. His head twists back, his eyes large and hollow with fear. I drag myself to my feet, douse myself in water from a barrel and run after him. I must survive this night. I must be there when Father returns. I must find Mr Kyuku.

The air constricts and tightens a notch. The north wind grows insistent, fanning the fires. To the west, houses flare like red lanterns. The firestorm sucks up oxygen, hatches lethal winds. Knots of wood swallows flail about above me, their white breasts flashing. An old man beats at his house with a mat soaked in water. As he lifts it to swing again, the windows dissolve. He turns towards me and melts like a candle into his garden.

Near the river a bridge collapses, water boils. More incendiary bombs burst. Debris drops out of the sky onto my head. When these B29s return to the Marianas and their doors are opened, I know the stench of our burning flesh will linger there.

I can run no more. I sink to my knees and collapse face down in a ditch. Fire and darkness pass over me. Wind-borne pieces of rubble scuttle like rats across my back. I nuzzle my face into the dirt to escape the fishy smell of fat burning in skin, of hair singeing. This earth is cool. I burrow down into it, roll onto my back and turn my face to the bruised sky. Overhead a heron drags wings of fire. My eyes follow it until it disappears. Glowing embers fall as softly as snow as I close my eyes and draw a white handkerchief across my face.

Hours later I drag myself upright. I am no longer afraid. My body trembles. I brush at my clothes, shake the soot from my hair and wipe my forehead with the dirty handkerchief. A tight, sick feeling spreads in my stomach. I wade a smoke river. Charred bodies lie with arms reaching out. Black shapes clog the canal. Someone walks towards me out of the grey. No one's running now. People lie mortally injured on the banks of the canal. Moving from body to body, I make my way through whole suburbs desiccated by the bombing. As the smoke clears a little, the city emerges as a burned skeleton and stands like a forest devastated.

Beside the remains of a temple, a woman lies naked in the dust, knees drawn up to her breast, head resting on a pale arm. Long black hair flows into an ebony pool around her white body.

Dazed and confused, I walk for hours along streets lit by dying flames until I reach our lane. Standing in its garden of naked white birches Father planted when I was born, the house remains untouched by fire.

Once inside, I draw my quilt around my shoulders and kneel on the mat. I wait for hours. Here, within these familiar walls, I am the last living being. From time to time I doze. Behind my eyelids are bones blackened like bamboo, corpses flowering, and everywhere, wild antelopes galloping.

When night twitches over into day, I wake with a jolt to the sensation of people sitting on my chest. I rise in a cold, dim light, seeking evidence of my existence. A cup sits on the table, holds the remnants of fragrant tea. I hear ghosts. I hear them breathing.

I look into Father's cupboard and draw out a silver case

engraved with his name. I smoke a forbidden cigarette. In the glass I see the time of my beauty, for this is the time of my beauty, this is the moment of my youth. This is the day I turn nineteen.

My blood flows backwards.

I pick up the cup and break that bright mirror.

Through ash on the glass, a sliver of Mr Kyuku's grey roof is visible. I wash my face in cold water, slip on my sandals and slide open the door. Am I the last of the living?

I emerge into a sterile white light, a birdless sky. The sun squats low. Everything is still and calm. As the sun gleams impotently through smoke, it reveals the ravaged landscape. Our house is surrounded by sheets of buckled corrugated tin. A bird's body, its bones bleached, lies at the door. The noise of bombers and fire has deafened me and sealed me off from the world. I stand outside time beside Father's Koi carp pond and gaze at his precious fish waving their red bodies in the deep water. I drop my fingers below the surface and feel their glossy bodies brush by.

My heart lifts when I see my neighbour. Still dazed, I approach Mr Kyuku who sits on the step of his house.

Carefully he grooms his fingernails. His face is black.

Mr Kyuku! I'm so relieved to see you. I thought I had lost you.

I reach out a hand.

Don't touch me! he shrieks and, turning angrily from me, scuttles inside his house and slides the door closed. I stand alone with my arms hanging at my sides. I put a hand to my mouth, kneel in the dirt and vomit smoke. I crouch, shivering, my torn fingernails at my lips.

As I mourn the lost world, the dead rise up and walk along the lane. Someone passes by. Someone disturbs a spider's thread. I hear a dull thumping and turn the corner to see a man beating his bandaged head against the wall of our house.

A spittle of black rain falls. I look up, mouth open to the empty sky. A light breeze lifts across my face. Upon my lips, I taste the sweet and silky ash of my ancestors.

December, 1946 Tokyo

Low aubergine clouds brood above Snow, a fair-haired Australian soldier who is part of the occupational forces. Just before dusk he makes his way down an unnamed Tokyo lane, his Nikon slung over a shoulder. The temperature's dropping and he pulls up the collar of his coat. A few flakes of snow flutter down and up like white butterflies.

A dark figure kneels near a large pond in the garden of a gabled house surrounded by white birch trees. An open book lies beside her. She presses seed into a couple of rough furrows scraped in the dirt. She pauses a moment, perhaps because the snow begins to fall more heavily. Wiping her hands on the white apron tied around her waist, she picks up the book. As snowflakes froth about her, she lifts the open book above her head, making a little shelter, a little roof. Her dark clothing, the white apron, the angle of her legs and arms as she holds the book. The curve of the pages under the hard covers. The smoothness of her cheek in the evening light. All of these things make him feel for the first time that he's arrived somewhere. Quickly he lifts his Nikon and fiddles with it. Through the lens he focuses on the composition: the gentle slope of the shoulders, the angle of limb and head, the contours made by the bone-coloured wings of the book above her dark head. Holding his breath he examines her lowered eyelids, the curve of her nose, the lips parted a little. Her otherness seems familiar.

She hears the whirring camera and turns her head suddenly like a deer in a clearing in a forest might when it hears the click of a gun barrel dropping into place. She finds the eye of the camera and impales him on her dark, glossy eyes.

His arteries constrict. He can almost smell the sulphur of a struck match, the blush of heat inside him, flames licking against the cold. The snow falls more heavily, enclosing them both in its white cocoon.

In one quick movement she sets the book on the ground, rises, walks backwards away from him into the twilight, her eyes not leaving his face. Then, as the last of the smoky light leaves the garden, she turns away. She steps up to the veranda of the house, slips out of her shoes, slides open the door, and without looking at him again, disappears inside.

He stares at the space left in the garden: a vacancy in air and light, a silvery-blue luminance, a pure reflection of snow radiating away from him. The pages of the book flutter as the breeze picks up. He enters the garden, retrieves the book and approaches the house. He knocks. After a long time the door slides open and she stands there frowning, her eyes looking directly into his. She crosses her arms over her breasts, her fingers touching her shoulders.

He bows. Hands her the book. She lowers her head a little in reluctant acknowledgement, but stops herself. She reaches out and quickly takes the book from him. Before he can speak she steps back indoors and slides back the door.

It is the particular shape of her silence, her face struck by the snowy light. But mostly it's in the way she turns her head beneath the ivory wings. For Snow, the question of why he has come to Japan is fully resolved in that one gesture.

Spring 1957 Blue Mountains, Australia

With Snow off in the city looking for work, Hana anxiously watches a wisp of smoke rise above the horizon. It thickens a little, becomes a white flag waving above the Blue Labyrinth, this place of soft light as sumptuous as an ancient weaving on silk, all undulating lines and fluid transitions of colour. The blue is startling - a limpid, oily haze bathes the unseen world, the impenetrable wilderness in the subterranean valleys. Rust-coloured angophoras are scattered here and there in the grey. Beneath the abstract patterning of the eucalypts, on the floor of the forest, lies a thick layer of dry leaf litter, bark and scrub.

Drought has flooded the country; the arid air has been foretelling fire for months. Lavender and orange leaves lie curled like old lips on the hard ground. Every day Hana watches from the house she has come to as Snow's war bride.

Clouds come to tease, then draw apart like curtains, revealing a seamless blue sky. Now the thin dark plume of smoke is fed by an unfriendly breeze that shifts abruptly and the fire makes its run, heads west.

Hana switches on the Bakelite wireless on the kitchen mantelpiece. Down in the Blue Breaks, the fire's jumped and moved further into the intricate pagoda ridge system that is the Blue Labyrinth. It's gaining speed where the ridges and gullies are steep and narrow and the dry sandy soil is deep with beds of litter. More smoke appears like a dark bruise in the sky and soon it's breached containment line. Water bombs at Kanuka Brook fail to stem its tide. Fire-fighters put in further lines all along the twisted ridge, taking a stand, drawing a line in the earth, building fallback options, steering the fire into dead-end gullies, back-burning up to the point where they meet the mouth of the wildfire. They try to control the rogue fire with their tame ones but the main fire head, unfettered now, crosses Wood Creek below the cliff-line and directly threatens the ridge.

Wispy-winged fireflies appear through rising smoke. The

Japanese garden Snow has painstakingly built for her lies animated by light and open to the world. At its edge a bamboo fence separates it from the native bush, acres of scribbly gums. Flashes of colour strike her as birds pass through the sharp red of new maple leaves. The whir and drone of insects stir the gingko tree. She pauses in the coolness of its shadow. In the warm breeze the cherry tree tosses white petals across the mirrored pond. Birds drop from the white limbs of birch saplings.

The huge stone-rimmed pond holds her Koi carp suspended in a liquid trance. She'd collected them gradually and, in a special book Snow ordered from Japan, recorded and painted the colours of each one on the carp outlines printed there.

Hana leans over the edge and the carp swarm towards her, greedy mouths with huge lips kissing the air, sucking noisily. Their scales are molten gold and silver. Her eye catches the glint of the metallic sheen of the rose-gold one, the sleek white body of the mirror carp marked with velvety black calligraphy. Her young saffron-coloured fish overtakes another clad in a rich brocade of red and gold tints. She sprinkles their food on the surface and they tumble over each other in their haste to gobble it down. She remembers Father's carp pond. She wonders if fish have memories.

The air's charged with waiting. Night spreads out across the land as the fire approaches. Veins of red oxide glow as great drifts of flame feed on the eucalyptus bark on the forest floor. Hana stands by the door and gazes into the valley where the wind swings and the long flank becomes the head of the fire, picking up speed. Ignited skin from stringy-barks is blown ahead, creating spot fires, petals of flame. There's a drop in humidity at the fire front and it jumps in speed and forms an elliptical shape, the long axis stretching in the same direction as the wind.

The fire breaks the next containment line, comes through the coach wood forest, the flames inflating with their own authority. Trees billow under the moon, the sienna colour of flame. Clouds of ash rise. The heat comes in brutal gusts, sucks oxygen from air. A huge plume of smoke and debris forms updrafts and downdrafts; the flames leap to the height of the eucalypts. Then the heart of the fire bursts in an angry orange ball.

Hana stares in horror as the fire reaches the ridge in a rushing flood. A white cockatoo, screeching like a siren, takes off into the wind. Silvery grey scribbly gums ignite.

Two ex-army helicopters appear above, lights just a weak

glare through the smoke. Wreathed in smoke, they battle the inferno with water buckets. Shoals of screaming black cockatoos pass overhead. The pitch of the fire changes and comes right up the road, a great fireball sucking up wind. The stench of fuel fills the air as a turpentine tree across the road becomes a giant candelabrum, all its branches ablaze. Then it explodes in a rocket of flame, spitting out gobs of fire. Birds, animals, insects, branches, bark and leaves, dry seed husks are thrown together in an incendiary mix.

Inside the house Hana's throat scratches, eyes smart in the smoke. Her skin contracts in the heat. She chokes on the boiling, stinking smoke, the heat snatching up the oxygen. The wind screams like a jet engine driving the crimson flood. She has a bud of silence in her ears. The flames jump from across the road and move towards the house, catching at the roof, guzzling at the eaves now, wanting to make a bonfire of the house, a pyre. A red wave blasts windows out. The box that contains her parents'ashes burns. These strange things from Japan: the flames refine their existence.

She presses a damp tea towel into her face and rushes into the garden. Above her a helicopter hovers like some gigantic prehistoric bird, its body casting a charcoal grey darkness over the raked gravel garden. Its spinning blades whisk air like an eggbeater. It swoops down, lowers a huge hose into her carp pool and sucks up the entire contents of the pond.

No, Hana screams. My fish!

With a last hiss of suction, the helicopter swings up and away.

In the morning Hana leaves the garden and walks to the top of the ridge dodging the small fires that still burn here and there. Remnants of smoke bleed into the polished black landscape. Smoke rises from the valley in pure white plumes. The pink sheen of the morning gradually deepens to blue then grey. Huge cumulus clouds are brilliantly white on top, their bellies flushed with deep, dusky rose. Below them, a long band of cloud unfolds, and rolls in waves across the sky. Spread all around her, in the Blue Labyrinth, is the black aftermath of fire, a forest of burnt eucalypts. A giant field of white ash lies like snow on the scorched ground.

Corpses of birds lie where they have dropped from the sky. Steam rises from the charred forest and shrouds the land. From far off to the south, blue gums thump as they fall deep in the gullies.

She looks back across the black earth to where a patch of pink lies in the middle of smouldering native bush, the only colour for thousands of acres. It's the Japanese garden Snow laid out with geometrical and mathematical precision. Hana catches her breath. From here, through aluminium coloured smoke, the garden possesses a dreamy, elegiac quality. It's completely intact, quilted with white petals of ash. She smiles to herself at the fact of its survival, a foreign thing like herself in native Australia. Her heart jolts as she realises that there is just a pile of rubble where the house used to be. Only the chimney remains.

A soft drizzle starts and the remaining leafless trees are inked blacker still. Currawongs sing homage to the rain sluicing down black trunks.

And then the rain stops. The morning sun appears like a red-rimmed eye. She hears an approaching roar and the helicopter reappears, spectral in this light. It hovers above her, casting about for remaining spot fires, live embers. Just as it drops its load of water, she looks up and sees them swimming down through the air towards her. A school of bright orange Koi.

lamprey

Aksel Dadswell

I make love to her outside on the night-dark shore with the storm in charge of sound and lighting. Its pyrotechnics drown the peripheral throb of music and merriment up at the house. Colby and I have better things to focus on, our knotted bodies slick with sweat despite the balmy chill. But as I move inside her, the combination of nature's tantrum, some anonymous synth, and drunken revellers creates a rhythmic soundtrack to our coupling. She moans and shifts, hands tiny bear traps digging into the meat of my back. I'm just one long piece of rippling sinew as I thrust into her for the umpteenth time and try to postpone the blissful climax. It's difficult, but I think about the black water, the flames, that *face*...and manage to stave it off.

She finishes with an arched back, her mouth a sticky suction against my skin, halfway between a kiss and a gasp. A minute more and I can't stop myself. I flood the gates just as the loudest thunderclap roars its approval overhead. Gotta love nature's timing.

We kiss softly, bodies all limp and spent, a string of spit connecting our souls. I exit her still panting and we lie side-by-side, sand sticking to our sweat-sweetened skin like sherbet. I'd lick it off too, if she asked me.

Our privacy is short-lived. Ryan stumbles down the beach, his clumsy footsteps preceding him. There's intoxication in his gait and voyeurism in his eyes, which flicker greedily over our nakedness. I grab my jocks but Colby just looks at him. She doesn't seem to care if he sees her all bare.

He plants his arse down in the sand with the nonchalance of the shitfaced. I feel weird letting him just look at Colby like he is, but I guess the half empty bottle of tequila swinging in his loose grip will erase his memory by morning. As if to confirm this, he takes a swig.

'Hey,' says Ryan.

'Hey,' says Colby.

‘Hi,’ I say.

‘Good party,’ says Ryan, face slack with the bliss of the inebriated. ‘Fuckin’ ace.’

I laugh, just at the absurdity of everything. ‘Well what the hell else are we gonna do?’

James and Colby laugh too. It is pretty funny. The world may have ended, but sex and booze still manage to stay front and centre stage.

Not all species of lamprey are parasitic, but they’re probably not as scary as their less morally discerning cousins. I read about them in the encyclopaedia I managed to save from Lisa, Ryan and Sam’s arson-based shenanigans. Whoever owned the house – sorry, *mansion* – before the proverbial shit hit the fan was clearly both a rich bastard and an avid reader, because the library is huge. Granted, most of its contents became unwitting fuel for my friends’ pointless inclination for bonfires, but I nicked a handful of lucky survivors: a set of encyclopaedias, a leather-bound copy of the Canterbury Tales, some unexpected pulp in the form of HP Lovecraft and Robert E. Howard. I’m still ambivalent about the quality of my orphaned books, but you take what you can get, right?

Anyway, lampreys. The parasitic kind like to snack on blood and tissue, as you do. They attach themselves to their host fish with a flat jawless mouth full of teeth set in concentric rings. After excreting an anticoagulant they drill into the host with a sharp bony tongue, and there partake of their delicious living condiments.

Not that any of that's relevant, but their mouths freak me out. I've had the odd nightmare, to be honest.

At least I'm both warm and well-read.

Ryan and Colby and I sit, knees all drawn up, three little pigs in a row, watching the storm as it flees over the dark sea. A joint passes between us. Lightning sparks up behind the clouds, making shadow puppets of the wreckage.

'Sam took a dump in the garden,' says Ryan, oozing a dirty wet laugh.

'Did he?' says Colby. I hand her the joint. She takes it between a finger and thumb so pale they almost glow in the dark. Chips of red garnish her nails.

'Yep, a big wormy one. I swear it looked at me when he was done.'

‘Wow. Did it talk to you, too?’ She takes a drag, holds it for a minute before blowing the smoke out of her nose. She glances sidelong at me. I don’t know if I’m seeing or just imagining I’m seeing the corners of her mouth turn up in a smile. I love it when she does that. It’s like a secret, a warm little intimate thing. Like watching a stab of lightning together as it blooms on the horizon, and we’re the only ones to see it. Just like Ryan with Sam’s turd.

Ryan looks disgusted at Colby’s suggestion. ‘Don’t be *stupid*, don’t be silly. *God.* If shit could talk then...then the world’d fall to pieces.’ He pauses as the irony sinks into his addled brain. ‘Oh. Woops.’ Another gurgled laugh. ‘Better go see if it’s got any last requests. He’ll be all dried up by tomorrow. I should give the poor fella some water.’

He staggers upright and meanders off to tend to his friend’s sentient bowel movement.

Alone again. Just us and the slowly repeating waves.

Colby hands the joint back. I take it, and lean over to kiss her. She tastes of salt and pot and sex. She’s still naked, and I’m as good as. Strange, how after everything we don’t feel vulnerable. We should be cowering in a hole somewhere like everyone else. Well, I *say* everyone. That kind of collective doesn’t really exist anymore.

Young people don’t seem to give a shit, really. The world could literally be falling apart around us, millions dead and all that, and we’d just keep on going. Partying. Drinking. Fucking. Being indifferent and awkward and a general irritation.

It is. We do. We are.

Colby nudges me, giggles. ‘Off with the fairies?’

‘Yeah,’ I laugh back, ‘give us a puff.’

She passes the joint back, its length shortened by her attentions.

While I take a drag, Colby gestures further along the beach. ‘It’s like a sculpture or something, huh?’

I cough out another laugh. ‘Yeah.’

Colby shrugs. ‘What’s left of it anyway. If there were still art galleries and shit, we could sell it for fucking millions.’

My laugh’s interspersed with weak coughs. ‘I s’pose so, if they were idiots.’

‘That’s a given. And, actually, I reckon it does look kinda cool. It casts cool shadows.’

‘I guess.’

I blow the smoke out and turn to the wreck. The engine is bigger than I imagined it would be. It barely looks like an engine anymore, all torn and twisted, as if its ruin were something effortless, easy as crushing a peach in your hand. I remember it coming down over the ocean, an industrial phoenix on the verge of rebirth. That sound, too. Like a screaming bird; terrified, frantic. An inferno of noise and light and death, in the end. Lucky we weren’t on the beach then. We heard it from the house and came running out to see what new impossibility the world had in store for us. In those terms I guess it was underwhelming. Just a plane crashing? You haven’t seen anything.

I saw one of them, one of the...things, right after the crash. We all stood there watching silently as it burned, and those few passengers not yet dead stained the night with their screams. The tail had landed in the water, and like the rest of the plane it too was burning. Corpses torn like confetti floated on the water. Apart from this eruption of death all around us, the night was still. The sky mirrored the sea. Colby had my hand in her bear-trap grip.

I was looking out at the water, the flames reflected in its ripples, and that's when I saw it. It was only for a moment, and I doubt anyone else noticed, but it was one moment too many. It didn't have eyes, or at least nothing that we'd recognise as eyes, but I knew it was looking at me. I suddenly wanted to vomit and cry and shit myself all at once. I'd rather have run a blade across my throat than have it look at me like that.

And then it was gone beneath the water, and my terror with it, and the world kept on turning. Or wobbling, I guess.

Whatever it was, it's hard to describe. Wet, shiny. Inky as the sea. Other than that I don't know what to say. It's like the manifestation of childhood terror. We don't really know what it looks like or if it's even real but we know we're scared shitless by it.

I keep seeing it in my dreams, in the shadows behind doorways, reflected in my friends' eyes. Either it's genuinely stalking us, or I've gone batshit. I wouldn't be the only one. I think most of the population went that way after what happened. I like to think of them as cowards or lightweights,

but I can't blame them. If you're dead or crazy you're one of the lucky ones. That's why so many more just killed themselves. Not being the dominant organism isn't nice for the ego. Our problem – young people I mean, adolescents – is that we never were. Our egos are both miniscule and enormous at the same time – a typically teenaged contradiction – so it's kind of hard to faze us.
Sometimes we pretend though. That we don't give a shit. Or maybe no one ever bothers to think that we do. I don't know. We're all people. We should know.

It's almost four in the morning. All that's left of the storm is a distant flicker on the horizon, the only thing separating sea from sky. The joint's gone too, just ashes in the sand and smoke in our throats. I don't even feel that stoned.

The party's still going on, the music throbbing, the people yelling drunken shit.

Colby looks at me, yawns.

'I'm going back inside.' She says. 'I need a drink.' She gets up, dusts the sand off her skin. Her clothes are scattered across the beach. 'You coming?' she says, pulling her underwear back on.

'I think I'll stay out here for a while. Watch the water.'

'The boy who loved his own company.' She smiles.

'Something like that,' I say, smiling back.
She leans down, presses her lips against mine. 'See you later.'

Her warmth lingers on my skin long after she's gone. I try to imagine making my way through his scorched world without her, and it's a painful thing. My parents never liked her, and hers treated me with a kind of grudging respect that never seemed to mellow. Always caught up in their own ideas and constructs, so sure of their straw houses and their straw lives. Now that's all gone; some of the first shit to burn up. Now, they're dead, and their opinions mean even less. Our youth shouldn't negate the feelings we have for each other. Specially not now, when those feelings are the only cinders keeping us warm at night. Those and dumb-arse metaphors, I guess.

I don't know what we're doing here. Not in a profound way. But this mansion. This beach. Are we waiting for something? Are we barricading ourselves in? Are we settling down to play house while the world burns? It has been for a while now. Burning, that is. I think the flames are almost out.

The sea's so dark. The ebb and flow of it endless. I can't get it out of my mind. It's waiting out there for me, in the dark between the waves. It's waiting for us all. It'll win in the end, probably. And once we're in its grasp it'll eat us, or kill us, or drink our souls or whatever it wants, really, and that'll be that. Or, maybe it won't. Maybe it's dead or gone or just indifferent. Maybe we're all mad and none of this has happened. Maybe it's just me.

Either way, we're still screwed.

why would you want to walk in such devastation?

Peter Hill

Diary Entry

May 29th 2012

3 months after the Babbington Fire

[Karri Island, N.E. Chudalup, Northcliffe]

A warm day – wind blowing. After days of unseasonably still, clear conditions.

An eerie sense of unease. A few birds can be heard – but only a few. The wind blows through the dry leaves that remain – fifty metres up. The rest have fallen to cover the unfamiliar site of bare earth in a Karri forest. Decades of leaf litter, understorey and humus have all gone.

The sound of twigs and seedpods dropping to the ground are not uncommon and fall harmlessly on my ears. It's the irregular spacing of a sharp, loud cracking sound that sets the mood. Like some polyrhythmic percussion played with a small axe hitting trees on a stage one kilometre wide.

From all quarters the thick bark cracks as the trees prepare to shed their skin.

The soundtrack of a forest racing to fill space created by fire.

Inside this Karri island, surrounded by sound, two-leaved seedlings and orchids emerge from the ash.

Home Again

'Why would you want to walk in such devastation?' she asks later.

Awe and wonder. Nature adapted to cope. Resilience.
Defiance.
The will to live pushing through.

A forest racing to fill space created by fire

Karri island NE of Chudalup, Northcliffe

An eerie sense of unease

Orchids emerge from the ash

Trees prepare to shed their skin

the alkali cleansing

Janet Jackson

In this forest I smell
the leaves, always the leaves,
their eucalyptus breath
But not today

Today I smell, dark but not dirty,
the alkali cleansing
of charcoal and ash

I hear not beaks, not bright feathers, only
the baritone wind
and my soft alto heart

I taste not smoke, not now, but fire-dust
surrounded and spent
in the wet film on my tongue

Rain is coming
I smell the negative charge
Rain is coming
Rain is coming and I feel
the fire-sprung seeds
making ready

alert message
north warrandyte, victoria feb.7th 2009

Karen Throssell

Dense inside heat, mounting radio tension
Learning a new language – 'Ember attacks' 'Alert messages':

The residents of the following towns are advised that due to increased fire activity in their area they should activate their fire plans immediately and remain on full alert:
Labertouche, Robin Hood, Acheron,

CFA CHECKLIST:
Fire plan to stay and defend:
Clean gutters, fill water barrels, check fire pump, rake leaves, rake again.

Uneasy quiet, whirr of fan and anxious murmur of John Fane on 3LO.
Wander, touching things. Stop, they're just things.

The residents of the following towns...
Churchill, Callignee, Jeeralang

CFA CHECKLIST:
Check batteries for torches, spare radio.
Shaking fingers can't get plus and minus right...
Raking, raking.

Sweat streams from me when I move from the fan.
Water indoor plants – Maidenhair shrivelling just from heat of glass.
Carefully remove tiny burnt fronds

...that due to increased fire activity in their area they should activate their fire plans immediately and remain on full alert:
Kilmore, Wondong, Beechworth

CFA CHECKLIST:
Buckets in every room, towels for doorways
Woollen blankets handy. Didn't fill bath yet,
no sense wasting water.

Laying out patchwork in semi darkness, keeps me from pacing.
Making a quilt from heirloom fabrics, mum's old curtains, dresses.
Keep each piece in tissue paper. You have to treat them really carefully,
or they come apart in your fingers.

The residents of the following towns are advised that due to increased fire activity...
Labertouche, Gindivic, Robin Hood, Acheron, Churchill, Callignee, Jeeralang,

CFA CHECKLIST:
Poke head out door, check for smoke and embers –
Oven blast of searing air, plants reeling in white heat.
Can't smell smoke – definitely no embers.

Stack dishes. Feel rough and smooth of handmade pots.
Favourite crystal –
(Dad's old whisky glass, mine now, but so *him*.)
Tuscan jug smuggled in as hand luggage. Touch it wistfully, stroking, stroking.

Sternly replace it. Just a thing.

...due to increased fire activity in their area and the possibility of ember attack...
Labertouche, Gindivic, Robin Hood, Acheron, Churchill,
Callignee, Jeeralang,
Kilmore, Wondong, Beechworth,

CFA CHECKLIST:
Check our fire clothes: boots, overalls, new gloves and goggles, masks. (Can't find hats that aren't straw...)
Sarong and bare feet for now — won't take long to change.

'...remain on full alert.'

Open the door again. Bliss!
Wind blast switched off. Heat there but bearable.
Fling open windows, doors, let the cats out, pour a drink.
Cool change — 24 tomorrow. It's all over!

Then I turn on the TV news.

'Marysville, Strathewen, Flowerdale, Kinglake, St.Andrew...'
(At 5.00 pm just before the wind change, fires were 15 minutes from North Warrandyte. When the wind changed from north to south west it turned the fires away and towards Kinglake and St. Andrews where 42 people were killed and over 500 properties destroyed.)

the pressure suit

Brooke Dunnell

Four months after the fire the boy went back to school, his arm and chest wrapped in a taupe-coloured pressure garment. An all-school assembly had been held the day before to prepare the other children. 'Ben is extremely brave,' the principal told them from the stage. Rows of bright eyes glittered up at him uncomprehendingly, their idea of bravery limited to vaccinations and getting lost at the supermarket. The principal cleared his throat and rested his left hand, then his right hand, then his left hand on the microphone. 'We need to treat him just like everyone else.'

The message was conflicted: Ben was special; no, Ben was normal. The next day when the boy emerged from his father's car, stiffened right arm held out to avoid bumps, the others could only stop and watch. The teachers on duty forgot to admonish as they looked for the man in the driver's seat, the shadow who'd barely been seen since the blaze took his sleeping wife and baby. From the veranda of the admin block you could just make out the grey-stained lower half of his face and the hands on the steering wheel, a perfect ten-and-two like a watch's smile. Other parents would be expected to walk their child into school after a long absence, but the widower existed in a grief-world now. The door shut behind Ben but the car stayed parked, engine turned off and the windows dark.

The principal hurried down to meet him, sweeping the limp schoolbag over his forearm. He went to reach for the small shoulder but stopped, remembering the tender pomegranate skin below the fabric. Splaying fingers in the air behind the boy's neck, the principal directed him up the path to the office, talking in low and fast tones to distract from the open gazes of the other children. A boy standing under a eucalyptus tree waved uncertainly, his face more fearful than Ben's.

*

In the utility shed by the staff car park the new school gardener threw bags of mulch onto a metal trolley. He'd started the job at the beginning of the year, assuming the trowels and rakes of a man who'd worked at the school since it opened but was now fighting the weeds of cancer that had begun to sprout inside him.

A week into first term the gardener drove to work under a layer of smoke. At first he didn't think much of it since the air had been sharp with burning smells since Christmas: bushfires in the national park, teenagers playing silly buggers in vacant lots. It was only when he went into the staffroom for a glass of water that he heard two off-duty teachers talking, their voices quiet with trepidation: a house nearby had caught alight in the early morning, cause unknown, and neighbouring parents reported seeing ambulances parked behind the fire truck. No one was sure who lived in the house, but somehow they knew it was part of the school community. The gardener held his empty glass in mid-air, the news sinking coldly through his skin. 'I double-checked my class list,' one of the teachers said. 'Two students missing.'

That day the gardener turned on the shed's portable radio every hour for updates. By midday they had confirmed the casualties: a mother and infant deceased in the house and a primary-school-aged son taken to the children's hospital with partial thickness burns. The father wasn't home at the time. The next morning the newspaper carried a front-page shot of the blackened half-home and an interview with fire investigators. A mosquito-repelling candle, lit to drive away the bloodsuckers that streamed through the sleep-out's louvered windows, had been placed on a wooden stool between the baby's cot and the mother's single bed. A younger son slept in the next bedroom and the father had already left for work. In the muggy, airless predawn, the candle tipped over. Flames ran down the leg of the unvarnished chair and over to the bed, shrouding the sleeping woman. Authorities reported that the baby's tissue-paper lungs had given out before his cot caught fire.

He read every story over the following weeks, keeping track of the funerals, the boy's recovery, the piles of flowers left outside the ruined property. The gardener wanted to keep these articles but he knew the fine line he walked with parents: a young male new to the area, working so close to their prepubescent children. He memorised the reports and threw them away.

The same day the boy returned to school the gardener drove past the house on his way home from work, slowing to look at the sign tacked to the temporary fencing: KEEP OUT. Immediately following the fire the unburned half had spewed the remains of the life it once held: a soaked sofa, a television covered in ash, red balls from a baby's mobile melted into puddles. Those things had been taken away — by the family, the gardener hoped, and not vile looters — and now it was just a grey-black shell, the scorched bricks on the northern side as desolate as long-extinct chimneys. In nature fire meant regeneration, but this one was unnatural and had locked its environment into stasis. A mausoleum for mother and baby: nothing could grow here. Eventually the structure would be razed and the block would lie branded and empty. The gardener tapped his accelerator and continued down the road.

*

Ben's return to the classroom was symbolic rather than practical. He was left-handed but that arm, while not requiring near-constant pressurisation, was still injured, his small hand a pearlescent pink from the intense heat. He tired easily and couldn't concentrate. His already watchful teacher became a mother magpie, ready to swoop if anyone went too close to the nest. His classmates stayed away, not because of the strangeness of the elasticated suit he wore beneath his shirt or the beady-eyed protection of the teacher but because of the misery that clung to him like smoke. They smelled it.

In the weeks after the fire Ben's father was at the hospital every day, popping in and out of the room as nurses swarmed over him to check the grafts. 'Just going down to the cafe, mate,' he'd murmur, then not come back. Sedated, Ben slept for long periods of time and woke without knowing the week, the day, the hour. At first he didn't dream much but later he started to see the burning cot in the dark and woke gasping, right arm electric with pain. His father held his unburned shoulder. 'Okay mate,' the boy heard above the low whirring of machines and the squeak of rubber wheels in the corridor. 'Okay.'

The funeral was held off until Ben could attend. Five weeks after the smoke muted the dawn Ben and his father were picked up from the hospital by a cousin and driven through the suburbs to the cemetery. The boy sat in the back, bandaged right arm on a stack of pillows, next to a tall woman he didn't know. During the service she stood behind Ben, her height and unfamiliarity making him feel like he was up against a wall. When they got back to the hospital Ben asked his father who she was. He was still in his black suit and stared intently out the window. 'That's the social worker,' he said. 'She's come before.'

The woman started to appear in his room every few days; sometimes when his father was there, sometimes when he wasn't. 'How are you feeling?' she asked, and he would say, 'My arm hurts.' She would nod and look down at the notes she held at her waist, an unimaginable distance from her nose. 'Do you understand what happened to your mother and brother?'

'They died in the fire.'

'That's good, Ben,' the woman said, writing something down. He wanted to tell her that it wasn't good, but in the hospital he'd learned to conserve his energy. 'Your body is growing new skin,' the doctor had told him. She was Indian and had a long nose like a tongue depressor. 'It takes a lot of work and will make you tired.' One day she came in wearing his mother's favourite perfume, and when he panicked she didn't wear it again. 'I know it hurts, Ben,' she said afterwards, antiseptic-scented and holding the silver bell of her stethoscope. 'You're an incredible boy.'

His dad said, 'Do you feel like you'll be ready to go back to school soon?'

The view outside the window was of the hospital's car park. Colourful, bulbous caterpillars were stencilled on the walls of his room, and they stared at Ben as he tried to sleep. 'Yes.'

'We can't go back to the house, though.'

'It burned down.'

'We could stay with Lou,' his father said, referring to the cousin who'd driven them to the funeral. Lou visited every day after tea, reading to Ben and massaging the crawling feeling that sometimes developed in his calves. When he fell asleep she brought his dad dinner. 'You've got to look after yourself, Terry,' she said, but Ben's father didn't know what she meant.

*

The boy had been back at school for six days before the gardener saw him in person. Returning his broom to the shed after sweeping outside the office, he saw Ben sitting on wooden bollard at the edge of the staff car park. The boy looked in his direction and the gardener didn't know if it was appropriate to smile. 'Hi there.'

'Hello.' The boy shifted his gaze to the rows of vehicles in front of him. His padded right arm lay across his lap, soft and beige as a Cabbage Patch doll's.

The gardener wasn't sure if he was meant to talk to the kids. It was probably better if he didn't. 'Supposed to be in class, aren't you, mate?'

'Don't want to.'

‘Got to go to school, unfortunately.’

Ben looked at him again. He cocked his shoulder to lift the injured arm. ‘I got burned in a fire.’

The broom was suddenly so heavy the gardener had to rest it against the aluminium siding of the shed. ‘I heard about that,’ he managed to say. ‘That’s very sad.’

‘But I still have to go to school.’ The boy sounded resigned.

Twelve weeks ago the gardener had stared at a newspaper photograph until its ghostly negative was printed in his mind. The camera had fixed on a boy in a crisp white shirt, the right sleeve unbuttoned to accommodate his bandages. In the foreground was a gleaming jarrah coffin, the flowers on top melting out of focus. The boy’s lips were thin as his teeth bit into them. *Mother, infant farewelled after deadly house fire.* The gardener tried to think of what he could say to soothe the child’s blistered spirit, but there was nothing.

Ben tilted forward until he slid off the bollard. ‘I told my teacher I was going to the toilet. She made Paul go with me.’

‘Where’s Paul now?’

'I don't know.'

He watched as Ben walked off. With his arm and torso encased in padding the automatic expectation was for the kid to limp and shuffle, but his legs had not been burnt. Watching him open his classroom door, the gardener realised what he could do.

*

Ben and his father were sleeping in Lou's son's room. When Ben got out of hospital they initially put the two boys together while his dad slept on the couch, but in the middle of the first night Ben went looking for the toilet and got into Jay's wardrobe by mistake, knocked his arm painfully against a hockey stick, and couldn't get out. The adults thought it was a great sacrifice that Jay had given up his room so that father and son could comfort one another, but really the other boy found it too terrible to see the crusty skin emerging from his cousin's shirt collars and the flinch as he was zipped into his suit. The weekend before the fire Jay had used a magnifying glass to torch dry gum leaves out the back, marvelling at the black-rimmed holes that expanded over the surface. Stroking a charred edge too soon, a slim white line seared the tip of his finger. For the next few days everything he touched had a double texture: normal on either side of the burn, and then a thread of numb distance no matter how hard he pressed. He wondered if it would scar, leaving a permanent stroke through his fingerprint. Then the rumour went around school that a whole family had died in a house fire and when he got home his mother was on the front step with her face in a tea-towel. Sometime after that the little burn on his finger healed without a trace.

Once a week Ben's father drove him to the hospital to see the doctor. Gently, gently, she unzipped his pressure garment. 'The skin is the largest organ in the body,' she told him, lifting his left arm to check underneath. The membrane covering his ribcage was a distended red balloon, its surface blotched and fragile. 'It holds in all the vital fluids. When the burn penetrates too deeply, they start to leak out.' She lowered his arm with her feather-soft fingers and looked him in the eyes. 'You must feel like your body is crying.'

*

At home Ben's father met with a man whose tie didn't match his shirt. They went into the kitchen while Lou and Ben watched cartoons in the next room. Ben didn't recognise any of the programmes. Two jewel-coloured elephants fought for the attention of a frothy poodle in a skirt, their gestures growing more and more melodramatic over time. At the end of the episode when she evaded them both they entwined their stumpy teal arms. 'Friends?' one asked, and the other agreed, 'For life.' The apparent catchphrase meant nothing to Ben. He was ancient now, stiff and weak like his grandfather had been just before he died.

The voices came through the wall; the man in the bad tie, who seemed to speak very slowly, and over the top of him Ben's father. 'Under the terms of your wife's Will, all assets go to you in the first instance.'

'I want the money to go to Ben.'

'You can pass them on to him in the form of a gift,' the other man said, each word drawn out like it was being translated.

'I'll give him the lot.'

'A lovely gesture.'

'I'm getting a payout from the insurance people and that's going straight to Ben, as well.'

In the lounge, Ben looked down at the synthetic skin covering his arm and chest. He felt Lou's hand on his knee but when he glanced at her she was watching the television forcefully.

'So we have to make it that Ben gets everything.'

'You're more than welcome to do so, Mr. Malone,' the man in the bad tie said, his patience veering on condescension. 'After the assets are transferred to you.'

'I can't take my wife's money.' His father was beginning to sound desperate. 'That's meant for Ben.'

'I think we agree, Mr. Malone.'

'I don't need it. I have money.'

His father hadn't been to work for three months. Lou did the shopping, wincing at the checkout as the sums added up.

'That's fine.'

'My son needs the money.'

'You can give it to him.'

'He lost his mother.'

Onscreen the two elephant friends fought over a pretty

octopus. Lou's hand squeezed Ben's leg.

'You'll get the money first, and then you can issue it to your son in whatever way you choose.'

'I'm going to give him all of it.'

'That's entirely up to you, Mr. Malone.' The rustle of chairs could be heard through the wall. The young man's voice came, slow and steady. 'I'm – sorry – for – your – loss.'

*

Jay usually rode his skateboard to school but today he strode silently alongside Ben, his thumb rubbing and rubbing the unblemished pad of his forefinger as if to scour the individual whorls away.

At the same time the gardener took a detour on his way to work. Old bouquets lay on the verge, stems and petals scorched brown by the sun. A new sign had been lashed to the fence, too wordy to read from a moving vehicle but obvious in its news: the house would soon be knocked down. The gardener barely slowed.

He saw Ben by the car park after recess. The gardener was carrying a stack of terracotta pots this time, cleared out of the junior school wet areas to avoid smashed clay shards. He stopped. 'Wagging class again?'

Ben glanced at him but didn't speak, his face clouding over.

'You still got fingers, mate?'

The boy looked shocked. No one had spoken to him this bluntly since he'd been zipped into the suit, his protection from the outside world. 'Yes.' He raised his right arm and wiggled the gloved digits.

'That's good.' The gardener leaned down to place the pots on the ground. Still bent over, he lifted his chin to look at Ben. 'I know it hurts and it's miserable and it looks really bad, but it'll get better.'

Ben stared at the man. He remembered the doctor at the children's hospital just after the graft, gazing down at him along the gentle slope of her nose. 'It will be all right one day,' she said, increasing his dose of painkillers. 'It will stop hurting.'

'I'll show you,' the gardener said, taking the ends of his

shoelaces and gently pulling out the knot. His fingers were tanned and nimble as he loosened the tongue of his left boot and slid it off, then peeled the sock away. His foot was very pink. The gardener rolled his pants' cuff upwards, the fabric revealing his leg like a raised window blind reveals a vista. The discolouration flowed over his ankle and halfway up his shin, where it widened suddenly and disappeared behind his knee. As Ben looked it assembled before his eyes; a shining stream of epidermal ruin, yellow ripples floating above the rosy riverbed. Near the nub of his ankle was a surge of bright red skin like a stilled wave.

'I've got no problems walking,' the gardener told him, rocking forwards and backwards on his leg to prove it. Bending over again, he ran a palm over the currents of flesh. 'Doesn't hurt a bit.'

'What happened?'

'Some petrol got on my jeans when I was filling up my motorbike. Then someone flicked a cigarette butt much too close.'

Still gaping at the scar, Ben began to run his hand over the sleeve of his suit, designing his own. 'Is my arm going to look like that?'

'Not nearly as bad,' he said, rolling his pant leg back down. 'That suit will smooth you all out.'

The boy said nothing as the gardener stepped back into his sock and shoe, then double-tied the bootlace. He straightened up. 'Better get back to your teacher, eh?'

Ben allowed the older man to walk beside him as he returned to class. 'Did anyone give you any money when your leg got burnt?'

'The lady who'd been smoking drove me to the hospital.'

'Oh,' Ben said. 'My dad wants to give me all of Mum's money.'

The gardener grimaced. 'I wouldn't know about that, mate.'

'But he needs the money. I don't know why he doesn't want it.'

'Money can make life easier,' the gardener said, thinking of the growing bills that had kept him from getting more surgery, the first layer of skin costing more than he ever imagined. 'Maybe he wants that for you.'

They had come to the Year Four classroom. The teacher saw

them through the window with her magpie eyes and tilted her head in curiosity.

Ben hesitated before going in. 'I think Dad's life is harder than mine.'

'It would be,' the gardener said softly as the boy turned towards the doorway. 'It would be very hard.'

They couldn't know just how hard it was. Even Ben hadn't gone into the trenches of misery his father was wading through. Even Ben, who squeezed his eyes shut at night to prevent fluid loss, hadn't experienced the lead pipe of unshed tears that plugged Terry from his diaphragm to his tonsils. Even Ben, who had stood, helpless, in the doorway of the sleep-out until the flames caught his pyjama sleeve, was not filled with the same guilt that circulated hot-cold through his father, who had seen the candle burning when he looked in on them that morning, but thought it would go out on its own.

quest for fire

Claire Dunn

Squinting, I survey my hand held out in line with the top of the far ridge and the setting sun. Four fingers. About an hour. Just enough time to find a place to camp and hopefully, make fire. I hobble downhill through the open stringybark forest, my bare feet sore from the long walk. I look for a circle of trees or some feature that I can temporarily claim as my own; something to mark the boundary of my camp. It has become almost superstitious, but it makes me feel safe. An old termite mound beckons me over, a burnt out tree squatting opposite. Like rusty bedheads I think, and tentatively set down my pack. I listen for a few seconds to how my body feels on this particular patch of earth. Good enough.

A flutter of nerves passes through me as I begin snapping dead twigs from low hanging branches. Even though it's been days since rain I don't want to take any chances with wood that's been on the ground. If by some miracle I get fire, I'd never forgive myself if it went out. I shiver at the real possibility of a long night without the companionship of flames, and employ martial art precision as I set the tee-pee fire one stick at a time. Needle thin in the centre, spiraling out to wrist thick on the outside, a small doorway left open downwind for the fire to enter.

The sun flings out its last net for the day, catching the bent backs of the tussock grass and staining them gold, like the web of the orb spider above. Turning my hat upside down, I begin making my tinder bundle; rubbing stringybark to a fine powder between my hands, plucking stamens from spent banksia flowers, crushing the seed heads of whiskey grass. I hold the mixture to my cheek to test for moisture. It's hard to tell, my skin cool in the dusk breeze. Twisting dry bracken fern fronds into a crude nest, I sprinkle in the tinder, pull a bulrush flower from my pocket for the innermost lining, the fluffy seeds soft as down.

All I need now is a spark.

I slowly begin spinning the straight grass tree stalk between my palms, grinding it down into a ready made notch carved on a thin board secured under my left foot. *First build heat, then increase pressure*, I remind myself. I resist the urge to speed up, keeping my hands floating up the top of the stalk, trying to conserve energy as the heat builds. Wisps of smoke curl into the air as I increase the pressure downwards. My arms and shoulders begin to ache. I grit my teeth. *The greater the need, the greater the result.* Hot dust fills the notch. I switch to speed, moving my hands as fast as I can manage up and down the stalk, smoke now billowing from the point of friction. *Come on, come on,* I say through clenched jaw. *You're almost there, just keep going.* My forearms start shaking. I grapple to control them but they wobble violently. I feel myself losing grip. The stalk jumps out of the notch momentarily, long enough for the hard-earned heat to disperse, and with it, any chance of a fire. I collapse, shedding hot tears of anger, just like the previous night, and the one before that, and the one before that, and most since I arrived.

*

I wake in the night cold and pull the blanket up around my nose. Without a watch I can only guess at what hour I have woken to. The kingdom of night insects is my clue. There is a point at which their symphony changes, see-saws back and forth like a DJ merging tracks, signaling the betwixt and between time when it is no longer night, nor yet morning. It is an empty time. Shifty. Stretchy. I catch it now in the insects' pause, as if recalibrating, settling into a new syncopated rhythm, fingers thrumming on a table. There is no going back to sleep. My heart stirs awake, squirms and thumps. It has its own rhythm too, its own language that I have been learning in the quiet hours when sleep abandons me to the forest's twitching hour.

Sighing, I swap hips and gaze up at the splinters of stars. My stomach growls loudly, reminding me I haven't had dinner. It feels like days since I woke this morning under a half-thatched roof, stuffed a water bottle, blanket, sandals, fire-kit, apple and sweet potato in my bag and padded quietly out of camp towards the hills. The walk was hard, scrambling through thick garnia and banksia scrub until it gave way to sheer slabs of rock and giant granite rocks stacked like popcorn on the cliff edge. Standing astride two boulders, I could just make out the Pacific Highway in the distance, a black snake in constant motion. The image shocked me, as if I'd forgotten that it was my choice to be barefoot on the ridge alone, not knowing where I was going to sleep that night, and not *down there* in the fast lane. Two different worlds, with me somewhere in between.

It feels good to get out of camp central though, have a bit of breathing space away from the others. It's been almost three months since six of us rolled up for the start of the year-long 'Independent Wilderness Studies Program' on the north coast of NSW. In some ways it feels like three years. Time's doing funny things out here. So far we've been kept pretty busy. Apart from building our own shelters from natural materials, we've been learning matchless fire-making, hunting and trapping, tanning hides, bush food, basketry, rope and string making, pottery, tracking, sensory awareness, bird language and navigation. The rules are few. Apart from no booze, we're limited to 30 days out of camp, and 30 days of visitors in. And that's pretty much where the structure ends. It is essentially a choose-your-own-adventure, with equal emphasis on simply experiencing the changing face of the bush, and ourselves, over four full seasons. A kind of cross between TV's *Survivor*, and the solo wilderness reverie elucidated by American poet and naturalist Henry David Thoreau in his book *Walden*. A chance to taste life in its purest form — 'Simplicity, Simplicity, Simplicity!' — as Thoreau exclaimed in praise of his self-styled life as forest hermit.

Easy for him to say. He didn't have to build his own shelter. He just moved straight in to a waterproof hut on the edge of a clear water lake, AND his aunt brought him cake every week (which he chose never to mention in his book), AND I'm sure matches were his fire stick of choice. Not that I'm complaining, this is what I wanted. I just didn't realise it was going to be this hard. My fingers curl in on the throbbing points on both palms where blood blisters the size of 10c coins rise up like red desert mounds.

*

SCRREEEECHHH! The piercing cry of a channel-billed cuckoo. It can't trick me now. The few times I dragged myself out of bed assuming it was calling in first light I ended up huddling in the dark for hours. It can't be too long before they take wing north to wait out the winter. I'll miss them. They remind me of home. Storm birds dad calls them. They were calling the morning I left for the bush, as if willing me on my way. I rose from beneath my pink childhood doona and walked to the edge of the garden, watching as the dawn sun cast spokes of gold onto the glossy black backs of the swans, perhaps offspring of the original swans that came to nest in the lake my parents created thirty years ago, the year of my birth. Packing the last of my things I turned back to wave at the two most familiar and constant figures in my life. 'Keep in touch,' mum called out, and then corrected herself, 'I mean, we're here if you need us.'

In my rear vision mirror they looked frozen in a photo mid-wave, dad with one hand on the collar of the family border collie, straining to chase me out the gate.

They tried to understand why I needed to do this. I didn't give them much to go on. 'I just need to get away from it all for a while, have some space to think, get back to basics.'

It was the same glib reply I'd churned out to anyone who'd asked. Partly masking my urge to say 'to get away from questions,' it belied my reluctance to try and put words to something that I didn't yet understand myself. Something that still only existed in feelings, in images; a river rock sculpted by water; an invisible hand tugging at my hem, urging me to walk until the city streets turned to dust underfoot and gave way to trackless leaf litter. Besides, how could I describe the sense that I never actually made a decision, as one might choose a car, carefully weighing up the options, but rather one day I turned over a rock to find a decision that I made long ago waiting for me.

Perhaps it was the first time I saw a woman kneel down and produce a glowing red coal with her own hands. She called it 'hand-drill', explaining it was the way fire had been made all over this land by indigenous people for thousands of years.

I was smitten. The sheer simplicity of picking up a stick and spinning it on another one to produce this incredible thing we call fire, was the most improbable and stunning act of human creation I could imagine. Pure alchemy. I couldn't take my eyes from her, from the fire she crouched next to, blowing and tending as one would a newborn. Within this new relationship she exuded a kind of quiet power, a connectedness. I wanted it, badly. That was three years ago. Now I want it with a bone deep hunger.

*

I sigh, and shift hips again, missing my grassmat. I might be failing at fire but at least I'm making progress on my shelters, having just completed the third and (dare I say) final layer of paperbark on my kitchen lean-to. Despite dreaming that the roof turned into a sponge and leaked torrents of rain, I ceremonially de-tarped for the first time last week, crossing everything that it's finally waterproof. I felt naked and vulnerable without the protective covering of the neon blue plastic, but less like an intruder, more in keeping with the camouflaged habitat of every other forest creature. More at home.

My real shelter is also taking shape, albeit excruciatingly slowly; grass bundle by grass bundle. I'm glad I stuck to my vision of a circular shelter. Some mornings I get up and just walk around it, like a monk circumambulating around a sacred mountain. Out here the idea of building corners and straight lines seemed completely out of sync with the circular shapes all around me — trees and raindrops and planets and berries and fly bums. I wanted to be hugged by my shelter, encircled by it; my own private universe, my own sun burning brightly in the centre.

It was important I got my hearth right. The first thing I did was to take a stick and mark its position, staking my claim. I dug a crude tunnel from this point to the planned outer edge of my shelter, hoping it will act like a kind of esophagus, breathing in air from the outside, breathing smoke up and out the chimney. Breaking the upper crust of topsoil I scooped out gravel and earth with my hands, hollowing a circular pit about half a metre wide at the top, sloped in to meet the air hole at the base. I dived down through layers of day-warmed water in the billabong to fish out chunks of pure white clay, spread it thick between sandstone rocks, massaging them in place with circular motions of my hands. I found the right fit for each rock, imagining where the billy might sit, the frypan. When I stood back to survey my creation at days end the whole area felt different, sentient almost. As if the shelter was already here, in spirit, if not yet in form.

There is only one way the first hearth fire is going to be lit. Hand-drill. My hand-drill. That I'm sure of. I'm beginning to fear it might never happen. I've been practicing every day, yet still sometimes can't even coax smoke out of the bloody thing, my shoulders and arms seizing up before I can even cut through the glaze. I've started a routine of push-ups to build strength.

'It's more about technique than strength,' explained the instructor Kate. 'You need to learn to channel energy up from your core.'

Kate held the board while I tried, witnessed my arms giving way, me punching the ground with my fists. She waited until I calmed down before saying, 'Even more important than technique is need. The greater the need the greater the result. Ask yourself, how bad do you want it?'

There was only one way to create need. I handed Kate all my matchboxes and vowed to use only primitive means to light fire all year. The others sniggered. 'It takes more energy to piss out here than most people expend in a day. We don't have to do it *all* right way,' said the Bear Grylls inspired bloke who could casually make fire while conducting a conversation.

‘All?’ I replied, seething. Fire is not just any old skill. Fire *is* life. I feel its potential within me, flickering, waiting, watching. It whispers promises. If I can bring flames to life, perhaps I can bring to life all that lies latent, all that has been yearning to flare.

Thankfully hand-drill hasn’t been my only option, otherwise I’d be pretty cold and hungry by now. I’ve found my stride with another fire-by-friction method called bow-drill, which uses a stringed bow rather than hands to spin the stalk. Requiring much less in the way of brute strength, the bow-drill was used by many cultures around the world. It’s a good fall-back but no substitute. For one, there’s no evidence of it ever being used here and secondly my string is currently a piece of parachute cord which feels a bit like cheating. No, I have to get hand-drill, and soon. That’s why I’m out here, with just my hand-drill stalk. Need.

*

The first *chip chip* of the eastern yellow-robin confirms the smudge of indigo appearing in the east. I can feel the soft underbelly of night at my back receding, curling up in hollows and burrows. The day nudges closer, wafts in like a mist. In the hangman’s light the kindling tee-pee stands straight and tall, expectant. Kate's words run through my mind, 'How bad do you want it?' I remember the look on her face as I held out my hands in reply, palms weeping blood like stigmata. She looked shocked for a second, then cocked as her head as if deliberating whether to let me in on some secret. Her words were slow, carefully chosen. 'You have to want it more than anything, but give up the trying.' The words echoed out into my confused silence.

*

I jump up, a sudden surge in my belly. Laying my fire kit and tinder bundle next to me, I peel off my jumper, and tie it around my head, drawing it down over my eyes in a blindfold. My fingers feel for the stalk, the board, find where they fit, find where my left foot nestles next to the notch. Pausing, I send out an impromptu prayer. I wince at the first spin, my blisters sending piercing pain down my arms. *Breathe, just breathe.* I focus on the rhythm of the stalk moving back and forth, the sound of wood rubbing against wood, grainy, gravelly. My shoulders loosen, surrender to the piston-like movement. *Keep floating, keep breathing. Nothing more to do here.* My arms begin to tire, and I pull back a little, visualise oxygen pouring into my limbs like liquid gold. I suddenly feel a shift, my arms gaining strength, instinctively pressing together and down, as if tapping into some kind of muscle memory. The sound changes, deepens. It is the sound of wood grinding to a dark powder, coalescing. Smoke fills my lungs and still my arms continue, up and down, up and down in fast fluid strokes as if cutting through water. A warmth in my belly surges up and out my fingers.

I pull off my blindfold in time to catch the split second when the hot dust spontaneously combusts into a red-hot coal. With my face mere centimetres from the tiny glow, I feel as if I could be looking into the eye of the Big Bang moments before explosion, swirling with the same limitless creative possibility, aroused by the same evolutionary drive for consciousness, for beingness. Perhaps it was this very force that brought me out to the forest, the same one that wills me now to transfer the smoking coal into the bundle, to hold it above my head as if in offering, and give it three long steady breaths of life. It flickers for a moment, then roars into flame. Shadows skip and sway through the forest. I rise, dancing to join them, dancing towards the dawn.

building fire

Moya Pacey

My mother takes an axe
to wood the colour of cold honey,
splinters, kindles,
twists last night's 'Gazette'
into paper sticks;
takes a match from the box
strikes and lights
the cardinal points
coaxes fire;
blows with lip-sticked lips.
Fire quickens...

My mother shows me how to trap
hot air.
She props a shovel –
blade rested on the iron fender,
drapes last night's newspaper
across its wooden shaft.

She makes a vacuum...

If there's no wood, she'll burn
old shoes – one winter
she chopped the upright piano
we played chopsticks on – piece
by shiny wooden piece –
What happened to the mystery of keys?

Fire ignites
spreads a singe of ink and paper
flicks a blade of flame
slashes the skin of last night's news.
Pull away the shovel.
The red of pure ignition.

the water tanks

Rachel Mead

She called them his mistresses
but he thought of them
as loyal mates in crinkled uniforms
looking out for the five of them
when topsoil and margins were thin
and water more precious than gold.
He repaid them in kind
with close attention
each day clapping their backs
feeling the cool compactness of water,
hearing the echo of emptiness,
gauging the corrugations of clouds,
and the Bureau forecasts for rain.

Two tanks for the house, two for fire
a squat squadron in formation
beyond the reach of branch fall.
The best insurance was preparation
yet he was trapped in town
when the day came
the front's ferocity razing every plan
wife and kids with no time
for the road or the sprinklers.
As the roaring dark swept over
they hunkered under blankets
in the tiny cross between the tanks
panting in the baked air
between those ribbed bellies
still cool and full, standing guard
among the fresh acres of ash.

black & white & colour

Mike Rumble

Synopsis

On Wednesday the 23rd November 2011 the controlled burn started in the National Park North of our home was out of control.

Strong North-Westerly winds drove a heavy covering of smoke down the coast and, combined with summer sun, coloured our sky with rich reds, gold and grey.

The natural beauty and power of the fire was humanised by the regular flights, at tree-top height, of the Helitack which refilled with water from a dam in the paddock just to the West of us.

As the evening approached the setting sun coloured the sea highlighting it with the same gold that had coloured our sky throughout the day.

After the fire passed and was brought under control the roads were opened again and we could view the devastation of the natural bush. Where natural colours of green and brown had been augmented by red and gold, what was left was black and white. The hints of green that were still visible turned to brown over the next few days as scorched leaves finally died and fell.

The only hint of colour was the exposed sand and soil mostly covered in a layer of ash but revealed in places.

Gradually the black and white was broken by new growth. In contrast to rich colours which had been reduced to shades of grey the monochrome landscape was now punctuated with bright spots of colour. This time not the red and gold harbingers of destruction but the joyous messengers of regeneration.

Nature reclaims its right to the land and its power to overcome the destruction of fire.

Wednesday 23rd November 2011–the controlled burn started in the National Park North of our home was out of control.

Wednesday 23rd November 2011–
as the evening approached the setting sun coloured the sea highlighting it with the same gold that had coloured our sky throughout the day.

Thursday 5th January 2012– gradually the black and white was broken by new growth.
In contrast to rich colours which had been reduced to shades of grey the monochrome landscape was now punctuated with bright spots of colour.

Margaret River Fires

In November 2011, the Department of Environment and Conservation (DEC) began a prescribed burn in the Leeuwin-Naturaliste National Park in the Southwest of Western Australia. The Report that followed, after the fires destroyed just over 3,600 hectares of natural bush and 38 properties, damaging a further 100 homes, described what happened: 'Sometime between Tuesday 22 November 2011 and Wednesday 23 November 2011, the Ellensbrook burn escaped its boundary and became a wildfire, running south along the coast to Redgate, some 20 kilometres away.' The fire had a devastating impact on DEC staff, FESA and volunteer firefighters, residents and the natural environment.

The impact on the natural environment is difficult to assess. Residents have noted that bird and animals have disappeared, and according to conservationists and animal carers, populations of highly endangered possums, black cockatoos and other native species may now be locally extinct in the Margaret River region. Margaret River veterinarian Michel Doney said possums were especially vulnerable to bushfires. 'They can't hop, they can't move fast,' she said, adding that she had treated about 20 possums for burns following the fire, and had been called out to euthanase a number of injured kangaroos.

Some months after the fires, Jill James from the Margaret River & Districts Historical Society and Niomi O'Hara from the Community Resource Centre in Margaret River conducted oral interviews with Margaret River residents.

Statements from these people focused on the unpreparedness for the fire and the confusion that followed. The question of whether to stay or go and the nature of this dilemma; the way one property might be lost while another right next to it saved; the terrible loss of wildlife and the bush were central preoccupations. The ongoing impact of the fire was also a major issue.

*

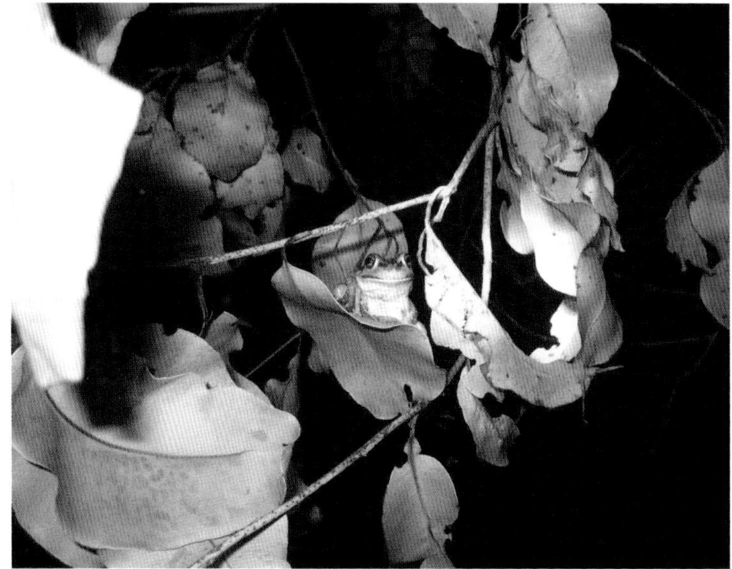

Photographs: Pam Hoyne

***Bill and Wendy Castleden* (Caves Road residents)**, thought they were relatively safe. On Wednesday, November 23rd, the fires were burning in Kilcarnup about 20 kilometres away.

When they came out of a meeting that morning, it was very hot, they noticed a large dark plume of smoke and they knew there was something wrong. They were unaware that DEC had re-started fires but the heavy smoked filled sky made both of them very anxious.

About six the next morning (Thursday) they walked up the track behind their property towards the ocean where they saw smoke in the distance – north of the river. When they went back up the hill a couple of hours later they saw huge flames, thick black smoke and the wind was 'buffeting, it was gusting so hard we had to hang on to the veranda post', they realized then that the fire was out of control. It was not long before the fire jumped the river and was heading for Gnarabar taking everyone by surprise. Bill says, 'the fire must have reached the Redgate sub-division within two hours'.

They received a number of calls during the day saying the area was under threat. Friends Nick and Donna came to help, Nick a volunteer fire fighter said he was going to stay and help save the house.

Wendy says she remembers this sense of panic as the messages to 'evacuate immediately' kept coming. Bill and son Sam had decided they were going to stay and defend. According to Wendy and Bill, 'the noise was indescribable, from both the helicopters and the wind.'

Donna said, 'Wendy you are not staying, get what you want to save and get in the car.' Then the message came through, 'it is too late to evacuate, stay and defend.' Wendy says, 'we wet the towels, moved the furniture to the centre of the room and rolled up the carpets.'

But Donna and Wendy decided to evacuate anyway. Wendy collected three pieces of artwork, the dog, some family albums and followed Donna out. As she drove away, she says, 'it was the worst feeling for me last year, following Donna, I thought I don't care about the house. The only thing that is important is life and I have left Bill and Sam behind. That is terrible. I felt really bad and I was very emotional.'

*

***Mary Elton* (Orchid Ramble resident)**
On Wednesdays, Mary picks up her grandson Spencer from kindy. When she got out of the house on Wednesday, November 23rd , she noticed it was very smoky and she became concerned, she turned on the radio in the hope of getting some news but there was none.

After picking up Spencer she turned the radio on again but was still not getting much information. When she got home she attempted to get information from FESA and a friend who she thought would know what was happening but no one was able to provide her with any information. At this stage she decided, it was up to her to start preparations

Mary started preparing the property. The first thing she did was fill the gutters with water, she says, 'it was so smoky and windy and it was difficult to work out which direction the fire was coming from.' She grew increasingly concerned. She spoke to her son, Adam and her husband Bob who said he would come home. She had decided to leave, 'why stay, it was too dangerous, but within a matter of minutes the smoke was so thick I was sacred and felt I could not go. I rang my son and said I was staying. Bob was surprised.' Mary started filling the bath with water and soaking the towels.
Some time later, her son Adam came home, 'I looked at his face

and knew it was not good, he said we have to go now! The property across the road was alight, we left everything, jumped in the cars, we looked behind us and our front yard was on fire, we could see the flames coming across, it was really scary.'

*

Salli Coppin and Pascal Camison **(Kilcarnup residents)**
Salli and Pascal's house was one of the first houses in line of the fire that hit Kilcarnup.

It was Salli's day off, her husband Pascal had gone for his usual run and everything seemed fairly normal . They went into town to pick up their daughter about 12.30 and when they returned it was, 'very, very smoky. We started packing our car up, with what was precious – paintings, paperwork, passports, and good clothes. We started getting calls from friends and we realized it was more serious than what we thought. By then my stepfather had come over and reported it was getting fairly serious and said we should probably leave. By this stage, the sky was really thick and red with smoke. We had made the decision some time ago that we would leave the house, given it is a wooden house surrounded by trees.

My husband was on the roof with the hose filling up the gutters with water. We had two cars loaded with gear and dogs. The road out of our property goes through a clear paddock, we did not realise until we got there that the neighbours were all there ready to go. The flames were probably at least 10meters high or more, raging out of the national park .

A fire truck drove in with two firemen who were in as much shock as the rest of us, they got on the radio and said the fire is in Kilcarnup, and then shouted at all of us. 'Get out! Get out! we cannot do anything about your houses.' Salli says, 'I was in shock, seeing the fire coming out of the national park, we thought we had lost our property really.'

Photographs: Sean Blocksidge

the return

Beverley Lello

South West Cape, the endpoint of a continent,
a protrusion on our map. We point to that tipped
contour. *We will go there again. Remember*
afterwards how the fires raged.

The regrowth has the hold of thirty years;
it snags and pinches at our struggling limbs
where once it snatched at ankles. Animals
have formed tunnels and sometimes we, too,

crawl on hands and knees alert for
tiger snakes, smelling the air fermented with leaf
and dirt and feel the tremble of the breeze
nudging the tops of this tough, resilient

vegetation until we emerge at the edge of land
and gaze down at a velvet sea, a trim of lace
beads of rock. This landscape is reckless: trees
convulsed by weather, rocks tumbling down.

Remember when the storm controlled the night
and our tent, ripped from around us, danced
to its tune, our white limbs contorted in the whipping
wind that wrenched and wrestled flapping skirts.

The memory unwinds snagging laughter in our voices.
Skeins of stories unravel on this high perched-cliff.
We have carried these memories with us
through the walking days and place them

at their source, this place upon a map which feeds
new growth and buries old and has no storehouse
for our tales. We leave them floating in the air
as we retrace our steps and make our camp.

playing with fire

Miriam Wei Wei Lo

1.

Everything that could be said about fire
leapt from her mouth –

blistering, inflammatory words,
hurt and rage twisted into a ball
and doused with petrol.

He walks through the fireball
and presses his own incandescence
to her lips.

2.

It is cold
we sit round the fireplace –
cast iron box with a window,
inside it, defying all logic,
the thing that can be seen
but cannot be held in our hands.

Oven-hot day,
devil-wind whipping the coastal heath.
We sit in our houses – boxes with windows.
Outside, the rising mushroom cloud of smoke:
the thing that can be seen,
but cannot be held in our hands.

3.

Great-Uncle's house: burning joss sticks
and smouldering resentments;
everyone sits down to New Year's Eve Dinner –
Hakka village food, every ingredient
imbued with tradition;
every word heavy with double meaning.

What did they give us, in those bright red packets,[1]
to spend on the future?

4.

Who inhabits this metaphor,
raising its temperature to flash point,
exploding it into meaning?

Who is the fire
that consumes at will?

The vehement flame of love
and the holocaust of judgement;
cataclysm of terror
and upward rush of hope,
throwing sparks.

I leap into this name,
knowing I will be burnt,
knowing I will be saved.

(1) Small red envelopes containing money. Traditionally given by the married to the unmarried as part of Chinese New Year celebrations.

5.

Another New Year spent away from home,
my father and my mother grow old
without me. Great-Uncle's children
repeat the Hakka village food, without the man
who remembers the village. In the funeral drums
they burn paper houses for the next life –

everything reduced to ash.

I sift all my longings into bright red packets,
pass them on to my children.

6.

Eight months after
the small Gracetown fire, the dunes
have barely recovered –
burnt out frames of shrubs and trees
pin down the landscape.

On the rocky slope facing the beach,
the line where the fire was stopped:
still clearly visible.

7.

What words are left
after consumation?

Love and Anger lying so close
together on the bed.

He whispers
and she exhales
the breath of their completion –
a small line of smoke
joining earth and heaven.

untitled

Maurie Roche

I will never forget my first bushfire in 1968 at Manly, Sydney. Recently migrated from Ireland. I was a 'New Australian' and unaccustomed to the intense summer heat let alone nature's fiery wrath. I watched in awe as the flames reflected into Sydney Harbour, dancing on the swell. The next day, I walked through the burnt out trees where the firefighters had extinguished the flames. There was no sound, no movement and no life to be found. The lucky ones had flown away while the other creatures found themselves trapped til their death. It was a solemnising event that still managed to rejoice by hurting no human and destroying no property. My first bush fire.

Since establishing my home in Margaret River, the bush fires come to us. In the summer of 2011/2012 Margaret River was spared but nearby Prevelly was devastated. No loss of life, but much loss of homes. This time, I found it hard to be anywhere near Prevelly for weeks afterwards. Disasters like this bring hoards to gape.

In my photographs I try and show my awe and respect for nature's fire. It's very much a part of our lives in Australia.

Contributors

Cassandra Atherton is a writer and lecturer in Literary Studies and Professional and Creative Writing at Deakin University. Her publications include a book of literary criticism, *Flashing Eyes and Floating Hair: A Study of Gwen Harwood's Pseudonymous Poetry* (Australian Scholarly Press, 2007), a book of poetry, *After Lolita* (Ahadada Press, 2010), and a novel, *The Man Jar* (Printed Matter Press, 2010).

Miranda Aitken has had work published in *indigo*, 1 & 6 and several Australian anthologies including *Scintillae* 2012. Her poetry was Highly Commended in the Tom Collins Poetry Prize 2006. Miranda is in her final year of a Bachelor of Arts in Literature and Writing at ECU Southwest. She lives in Margaret River, works at the local bookshop and experienced the fire of 2011.

Sean Blocksidge is a local Margaret River resident and is the owner operator of the Margaret River Discovery Company. Sean is a Margaret River volunteer fire fighter. His photos in the collection were taken during the 2011 Margaret River bush fires.

Aksel Dadswell is currently studying a Bachelor of Arts with a major in writing and literature at Edith Cowan University in Bunbury. He has won a number of awards including the John Marsden Poetry & Short Story Prize for Young Australian.

Claire Wren Dunn is a freelance journalist, barefoot explorer and writer based in the Hunter Valley of NSW. She is currently working on a memoir 'My Wild Heart' about the year she lived in the bush without matches.

Brooke Dunnell has had her work published in *Meanjin, Westerly, New Australian Stories and Best Australia Stories.*

Jo Gardiner lives in the Blue Mountains. Her novel *The Concerto Inn* was published by UWA Press in 2006.

Carmel Macdonald Grahame has had her work published in *Westerly, Southerly,* and *Quadrant* among other literary journals – short fiction, essays and poetry.

Paul Hetherington lives in Canberra, having spent much of his life in Western Australia. He has previously published seven full-length collections of poetry, including the verse novel, *Blood and Old Belief* and two poetry chapbooks. His poetry has won a number of prizes and is part of the online Australian Poetry Library. He was one of the founding editors of the online journal *Axon: Creative Explorations* (2011–). He is Associate Professor of Writing at the University of Canberra .

Peter Hill is a visual artist who lives near the southwest town of Northcliffe in Western Australia. How we as people relate to the history of this land, our connection, interests Peter and is the main influence in his recent artworks.

Pam Hoyne and her husband have a six-acre bush block at Redgate in Margaret River. Pam's photographs were taken on their property shortly after the fires and were selected for a fire exhibition in Margaret River in December 2012. Pam's main interest is in photographing wildlife, the beauty of nature and recording family events.

Janet Jackson's publications include a collection (*Coracle*, 2009), zines and chapbooks including 'q finger' (PressPress), and a micro-collection in 'Performance Poets' (forthcoming, Fremantle Press).

Judy Johnson has published three poetry collections, a verse novel *Jack* and a novel *The Secret Fate of Mary Watson.*

Jack won the Victorian Premier's Award for Poetry and her second collection *Nomadic* won the Wesley Michel Wright Prize. Individual poems have won major prizes, including the Josephine Ulrick, Val Vallis, Bruce Dawe and John Shaw Neilson.

Michelle Leber is an award-winning poet, based in Melbourne. Her work has been published in *The Age*, *Sydney Sun Herald*, *Meanjin*, *Southerly* and *The Best Australian Poems* in 2009 and 2010 (Black Inc). She won the Bayside Poets Prize in 2011.

Beverley Lello won first prize in four short story competitions in 2011/2012: Albury City Short Story Competition, the Stringybark Fiction Award, Margaret River Short Story Competition and the Country Style Short Story Competition. Her poem, 'Crossing the Nullarbor' was published in *fourW twenty-two* in 2011

Miriam Wei Wei Lo As she approaches 40, Miriam is more certain than ever that what she wants out of art is meaning and beauty. Miriam studied writing at the universities of Western Australia and Queensland. Her first poetry collection *Against Certain Capture* won the 2005 WA Premier's Prize. Her collection *No Pretty Words* was published by Picaro Press in 2010. She has lived in Margaret River, with her family, for nearly five years and hopes that something of the place is beginning to show in her writing.

Donna Mazza is the coordinator of the Bachelor of Arts program at ECU South West. She was awarded the TAG Hungerford Award for her novel *The Albanian* which was published by Fremantle Press in 2007.

Rachel Mead's short collection of poems, *Sliding down the belly of the world,* was published by Wakefield Press; her manuscript *The Sixth Creek,* was both awarded a Varuna Publisher Fellowship with Picaro Press and shortlisted for the 2012 Adelaide Festival Literature Awards unpublished manuscript prize. Her poetry has been published in *Meanjin, Westerly, Wet Ink, Going Down Swinging, FourW* and the *Australian Poetry Members Anthology*

David Milroy's family links are with the Injibarndi and Palku people of the Pilbara. Formerly Artistic Director of Yirra Yaakin Noongar Theatre, his writing/directing credits include: *King Hit, Runumuk, One Day in '67* and *No Shame.* He provided musical direction for *Sistergirl* and *Dead Heart* (Black Swan Theatre Company) and Perth Theatre Company's production of *Wild Cat Falling*. He co-wrote and directed

Sally Morgan's hit play *Cruel Wild Woman* and Barking Gecko's production of *Own Worst Enemy* for the Festival of Perth.

Françoise van der Plank is an avid reader and writer. Apart from many other interests, she is an active member of the local CFA and experienced at first hand the big Grampians fire of 2006.

Kate Rizzetti writes and lives in Melbourne. In 2011 her short story, *Cool Change*, won the Southern Cross literary award. She has had a number of other works highly commended and published since 2009.

Maurie Roche started photography 18 years ago. He moved to Margaret River 15 years ago for the lifestyle. 'Living in the South West is a photographer's dream come true'. Maurie's main interest is in people and the landscape and the odd cow.

Mike Rumble is a local Redgate resident who experienced the fear, devastation and beauty resulting from the escaped controlled burn of November 2011 in Margaret River. As an amateur photographer for many years this is the first time he has shared his photographs publicly.

Dorothy Simmons is currently studying for a PhD in Creative Writing at Melbourne University. She was a finalist in the 2011 Scribe Fiction Prize. Her short story *The Notorious Mrs. K* was published in the *Best Australian Stories* 2010.

Sharon Tassicker has had a life long passion for the arts. She has held the positions of Co-ordinator of the East Kimberley Art Award, Assistant to the Director at the Lawrence Wilson Art Gallery at The University of Western Australia and Director of the Holmes à Court Gallery at East Perth. She is currently Collection and Exhibitions Manager, Janet Holmes à Court Collection.

Karen Throssell has had three collections of poetry published—*The Old King and other poems* (2003),*Remembering how to cry* (2004) and *Chain of Hearts* (2012). Her poetry has been published in *Overland, Quadrant*, POAM and *Artstreams*, and her poems appear monthly in her local Warrandyte paper, *The Warrandyte Diary.*

Heidi Trudinger is an artist living and working in North East Victoria. She holds a Bachelor of Fine Arts from Curtin University, Perth 1990 and Masters of Art from CalArts, USA, 1995.

Acronyms

CFA : Country Fire Authority

DEC: Department of Environment and Conservation

FESA : Fire and Emergency Services Authority

SES : State Emergency Service

Photograph: Sean Blocksidge

Recommended Reading

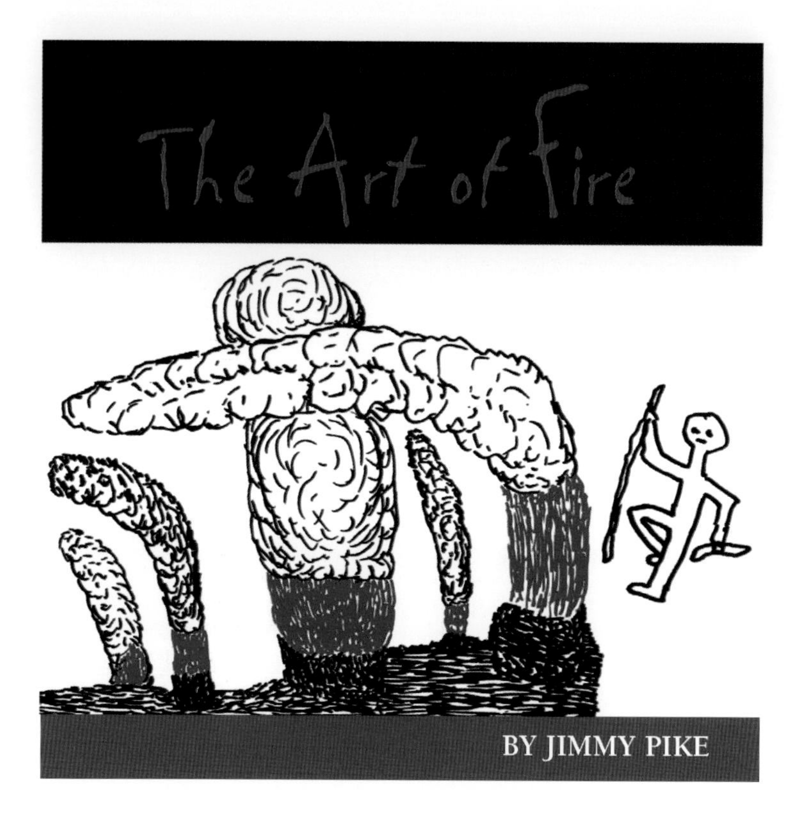

Australia is a land of fire. Fire has shaped its landscapes and played a role in the evolution of its plants and animals. Aboriginal people have always made and managed fire, in the domestic hearth and as an aid to hunting. This is both a book of art and a first-hand account of desert people's understanding and use of fire in inland Australia. The author, a renowned artist from the Great Sandy Desert, shows, through his minimalist drawings and compact, vivid descriptions, how desert people make fire and when and why they burn.

Available from Backroom Press, www.backroompress.com.au